I Asked For Wonder

I ASKED FOR WONDER

A Spiritual Anthology

Abraham Joshua Heschel

Edited and with an Introduction by
SAMUEL H. DRESNER

CROSSROAD · NEW YORK

This Printing: 2003

The Crossroad Publishing Company
370 Lexington Avenue, New York, NY 10017

Printed in the United States of America

Library of Congress Catalog Card Number: 83-072081
ISBN: 0-8245-0542-5

Contents

Introduction

Let us begin at the end.

Several years before Abraham Heschel's death in 1972, he suffered a near fatal heart attack from which he never fully recovered. I traveled to his apartment in New York to see him. He had gotten out of bed for the first time to greet me, and was sitting in the living room when I arrived, looking weak and pale. He spoke slowly and with some effort, almost in a whisper. I strained to hear his words.

"Sam," he said, "when I regained consciousness, my first feelings were not of despair or anger. I felt only gratitude to God for my life, for every moment I had lived. I was ready to depart. 'Take me, O Lord,' I thought, 'I have seen so many miracles in my lifetime.' "

Exhausted by the effort, he paused for a moment, then added: "That is what I meant when I wrote [in the preface to his book of Yiddish poems]:

" 'I did not ask for success; I asked for wonder. And You gave it to me.' "

"*Khob gebetn vunder anshtot glik, un du host zey mir gegebn.*"

Leaving Heschel's home, I walked alone, in silence, aimlessly, oblivious of others, depressed by the knowledge that the man who meant so much to so many was mortally ill.

I pondered his words. What had he meant by them? Was

it possible to accept death so easily? Death. Faceless enemy, fearsome monster who devours our days, confounds the philosopher, silences the poet, and reduces the mighty to offering all their gold, in vain, for yet another hour! Was he telling me not to sorrow overmuch, thinking of my feelings when he was moving toward the end of all feeling? Could he have been consoling me?

Suddenly there rang in my mind the striking passage with which he had concluded his first major work, *Man Is Not Alone*:

> Our greatest problem is not how to continue but how to return. "How can I repay unto the Lord all his bountiful dealings with me?" (Psalms 116:12). When life is an answer, death is a home-coming.
>
> The deepest wisdom man can attain is to know that his destiny is to aid, to serve. . . . This is the meaning of death: the ultimate self-dedication to the divine. Death so understood will not be distorted by the craving for immortality, for this act of giving away is reciprocity on man's part for God's gift of life.
>
> For the pious man it is a privilege to die.

And I found myself recalling a hasidic teaching he often quoted. "There are three ascending levels of how one mourns: With tears—that is the lowest. With silence—that is higher. And with a song—that is the highest."

I understood then what it was I had experienced: the lesson that how a man meets death is a sign of how he has met life. Intimations of melody countered my sadness. At that moment the power of the human spirit, mortal and frail though it is, never seemed so strong.

Ten days before his death Heschel had taped a television interview for NBC and was asked by the interviewer at the close of the program if he had a special message for young people. He nodded his head and seemed to turn to the future he would never see. "Remember," he said, "that there is meaning beyond absurdity. Know that every deed counts, that every word is power. . . . Above all, remember that you must build your life as if it were a work of art. . . ."

The day before his death, Heschel insisted upon traveling to Connecticut to stand outside a federal prison in the freezing snow, waiting for the release of a friend, a priest, who had been jailed for civil protest.

He died on the Sabbath eve, in his sleep, peacefully, with a "kiss," as the ancient rabbis describe the death of those who die on that day. At his beside were two books: one a hasidic classic, the other a work on the war in Vietnam. The combination was symbolic. The two books represented two different worlds: eternal spirit and mundane present, mysticism and diplomacy, heaven and earth. Most choose one or the other. Heschel refused to ignore either, preferring to live in the tension of that polarity.

After the close of the Sabbath and before the funeral a strange gathering of friends collected in his home to comfort the family: there were several former students, a hasidic rabbi, an esteemed writer on the holocaust, a well-known Catholic priest, and his last disciple, the son of the founder of a Japanese Christian sect.

How to mourn? with tears, with silence, with a song?

Who was Rabbi Abraham Joshua Heschel?

Born in Warsaw, Poland, in 1907, a descendent of an illustrious line of hasidic rabbis, even from early childhood Heschel was viewed with great expectations. At the age of four or five scholars would place him on a table and interrogate him for the surprising and amusing answers he would give. When his father died during his ninth year, there were those who wanted the young boy to succeed him almost at once. He had already mastered many of the classical religious texts; he had begun to write; and the words he spoke were a strange combination of maturity and youth. The sheer joy he felt as a child, so uncontainable at times that he would burst out in laughter when he met a good friend in the street, was later tamed into an easy sense of humor that added to his special personal charm. But there was also astounding knowledge, keen understanding, and profound feeling: an awareness that man dwells on the tangent of the infinite, within the holy dimension; that the life of man is part of the life of God. Some hasidic leaders felt that in him a renewal of their movement, which had grown dormant in the twentieth century, might come about. Others too were aware of the new light that was glowing in their midst. It can be said with certainty that the years in Warsaw provided that nourishment of spirit and intellect, that inner dignity of who he was, which gave permanent direction to Heschel's being. It could not, however, prevent him from peering beyond and, in the end, setting out from his home to explore the world of Western civilization which thundered and glittered about him. Departing from Warsaw in his teens, he traveled first to Vilna, where he pursued his secular education and joined a promising group of young Yiddish poets; then on to Berlin, the metropolis of science and philosophy in the twenties, where he immersed himself in the culture of the West and began to publish his first books and establish his career. For a short time he succeeded Martin Buber in Frankfurt, but was soon forced to flee the encroaching Nazi horde, by way of Poland and England, to America. The burden of his years in the United States were spent at the Jewish Theological Seminary in New York City, where from his small, crowded study, a series of major works emanated to a growing number of readers in America and beyond.

In Eastern Europe Heschel acquired his ancestral Jewish learning and piety; in Berlin, philosophy, method, and European culture; in America, within the blessings of the free society which he treasured, the full extent of his powers was reached. But regardless of where he traveled, Heschel's steps were ever pointed toward the Holy Land, and whatever the city in which he lived, his home was always Jerusalem.

Our age is one where men know more and more about less and less. Heschel's genius embraced a number of fields. He wrote seminal works on the Bible, the Talmud, medieval thought, philosophy, theology, hasidism, and contemporary moral problems. He was a theologian, a poet, a mystic, a social reformer, and a historian. Indeed, the best of the whole tradition of Israel, its way of thought and life, found a unique synthesis in him. Rooted in the most authentic sources of Israel's faith, Heschel's audience reached beyond creedal boundaries. He was easily the most respected Jewish voice for Protestants and Catholics: his friendship with Reinhold Niebuhr was memorable and his crucial role at Vatican II has yet to be described. A token of the esteem in which Catholics held Heschel, among the tributes accorded him after his death in 1972, was an entire issue of *America* magazine devoted to his memory, unusual in any case and duplicated for no other Jew. The years since his passing, far from dimming his person, cast in even brighter relief the unique role he played on the contemporary scene, a role no Jew, or Gentile for that matter, has since filled.

A master of English prose, though he knew little of that language when he arrived in America in 1939, Heschel, like his hasidic forebearers, had the gift of combining profundity with simplicity. He found just the right word not only to express what he thought but to evoke what he felt, startling the mind and delighting the heart as well as addressing and challenging the whole person. There are passages in this collection which, once encountered, will be taken up again and again, until they are absorbed into one's inner life.

Reading Heschel is to peer into the heart of that rarest of human phenomena, the holy man. For he was one of those who experienced the presence and the power of the living God, before Whom he walked both in the cloistered seclusion of prayer and study, and in the very maelstrom of our society. To Heschel the question of religion is not "what man does with his solitude," but "what man does with the presence of God": how to think, feel, act; how to live in a way which is compatible with our being a likeness of God; how to *be* what one *is*; how to so conduct ourselves that our lives can be an answer to God's question. Driven from the scholar's study by the very words of the prophets he pondered, Heschel suddenly found himself amidst the burning social issues of the time. Vietnam, civil rights, racism, poverty, Russian Jewry, Israel—all were agonizing objects of his concern to the sacrifice of his own research. He became a "commanding voice" on behalf of the "plundered poor." As with Amos and Jeremiah, "God was raging in his words." Indeed, after an encounter with him, it was not unusual for people to come away with the feeling that one of the prophets of Israel had suddenly risen up before them. He wrote what he thought and lived what he wrote. To Heschel, wonder leads to piety, and piety to holy deeds; for without the deed, wonder and piety are incomplete. And the deed, he taught, is always possible because man is not alone; God is ever in search of him.

"Emblazoned over the gates of the world in which we live

is the escutcheon of the demons. The mark of Cain in the face of man has come to foreshadow the likeness of God." So Heschel wrote while still living in Hitler's Germany. The nineteenth century saw the shaking of the foundations of faith in God. We who dwell in the twentieth century are experiencing the collapse of faith in the rival who was to replace Him: man. Poets applaud the absurd, novelists explore the decadent, and men prostrate themselves before the deities of lust and power. Our obsession is with human flesh. The ghoul who devours it is the latest film craze; the science of feeding it, firming it up, and preparing it for fornication, the most popular theme in literature. Daily we are bombarded by lurid reports on the mass-killer, the rapist, and the corrupt bureaucrat. The fantasies of even little children are now peopled with perverts and the radiated dead. Who will speak of those who do justice, love mercy, and walk humbly? At such a time we need nothing so much as to be reminded of the divine image in which we are framed, of man's purpose on earth. I am aware of no writer who has done this more powerfully, more eloquently, and more convincingly than Rabbi Abraham Joshua Heschel.

He knew he was the descendent of a people who ever since Sinai was destined to "dwell apart" and whose vocation was to be a witness to the living God amidst all the idolatries of history. Because he was spared from the flames which devoured his family, his community, and that whole irreplaceable world of learning and piety in Eastern Europe which alone could have produced him, he felt a special "burden" had been placed upon his shoulders. It was to remind men, with a testimony all the more convincing since it came from one who had experienced the fullness of evil, that despite the absurd and the apathy, the world is filled with mystery, meaning, and mercy, with wonder, joy, and fulfillment; that men have the power to do God's will, and that the divine image in which we are made, though distorted, cannot be obliterated. In the end, the likeness of God will triumph over the mark of Cain.

Heschel's writing is an embarrassment of riches. So compelling are his sentences that a paragraph literally chokes from wealth. One reader, overwhelmed by this plenty, suggested studying Heschel like a page of the Talmud, that is, weighing with care each sentence, each phrase, each word.

To allow the reader to stand still and dwell upon a word, or a phrase, or a sentence, that he might better taste the whole wheat of Heschel's thought, in contrast to the sustained thinking of his writings, and following the adage that less is more, I have at times restructured the printed page toward this end.

This book is an act of gratitude to God for the vision and the way of Abraham Heschel.

Samuel H. Dresner

I Asked For Wonder

GOD

God is of no importance
unless He is of supreme importance.

Ineffable

The search of reason ends at the shore of the known; on the immense expanse beyond it only the sense of the ineffable can glide. It alone knows the route to that which is remote from experience and understanding. Neither of them is amphibious: reason cannot go beyond the shore, and the sense of the ineffable is out of place where we measure, where we weigh.

We do not leave the shore of the known in search of adventure or suspense or because of the failure of reason to answer our questions. We sail because our mind is like a fantastic seashell, and when applying our ear to its lips we hear a perpetual murmur from the waves beyond the shore.

Citizens of two realms, we all must sustain a dual allegiance: we sense the ineffable in one realm, we name and exploit reality in another. Between the two we set up a system of references, but we can never fill the gap. They are as far and as close to each other as time and calendar, as violin and melody, as life and what lies beyond the last breath.

To Mock the Dawn

We can never sneer at the stars, mock the dawn or scoff at the totality of being. Sublime grandeur evokes unhesitating, unflinching awe. Away from the immense, cloistered in our own concepts, we may scorn and revile everything.

But standing between earth and sky, we are silenced by the sight. . . .

Heavy with Wonder

To become aware of the ineffable is to part company with words. . . . The tangent to the curve of human experience lies beyond the limits of language. The world of things we perceive is but a veil. Its flutter is music, its ornament science, but what it conceals is inscrutable. Its silence remains unbroken; no words can carry it away.

Sometimes we wish the world could cry and tell us about that which made it pregnant with fear-filling grandeur.

Sometimes we wish our own heart would speak of that which made it heavy with wonder.

2

Awe

Awe is an intuition for the dignity of all things, a realization that things not only are what they are but also stand, however remotely, for something supreme.

Awe is a sense for the transcendence, for the reference everywhere to mystery beyond all things. It enables us to perceive in the world intimations of the divine, . . . to sense the ultimate in the common and the simple; to feel in the rush of the passing the stillness of the eternal. What we cannot comprehend by analysis, we become aware of in awe.

The Horizon of Knowledge

We are rarely aware of the tangent of the beyond at the whirling wheel of experience. In our passion for knowledge, our minds prey upon the wealth of an unresisting world and, seizing our limited spoils, we quickly leave the ground to lose ourselves in the whirlwind of our own knowledge.

The horizon of knowledge is lost in the mist produced by fads and phrases. We refuse to take notice of what is beyond our sight, content with converting realities into opinions, mysteries into dogmas and ideas into a multitude of words. What is extraordinary appears to us as habit, the dawn a daily routine of nature.

But time and again we awake. In the midst of walking in the never-ending procession of days and nights, we are suddenly filled with a solemn terror, with a feeling of our wisdom being inferior to dust. We cannot endure the heart-breaking splendor of sunsets. Of what avail, then, are opinions, words, dogmas?

In the confinement of our study rooms our knowledge seems to us a pillar of light. But when we stand at the door which opens out to the infinite, we realize that all concepts are but glittering motes that populate a sunbeam.

A Song for God

He who chooses a life of utmost striving for the utmost stake, the vital, matchless stake of God, feels at times as though the spirit of God rested upon his eyelids—close to his eyes and yet never seen.

He who has realized that sun and stars and souls do not ramble in a vacuum will keep his heart in readiness for the hour when the world is entranced.

For things are not mute:

the stillness is full of demands, awaiting a soul to breathe in the mystery that all things exhale in their craving for communion.

Out of the world comes a behest to instill into the air a rapturous song for God,

to incarnate in stones a message of humble beauty,

and to instill a prayer for goodness in the hearts of all men.

Palimpset

We do not have to discover the world of faith; we only have to recover it. It is not a terra incognita, an unknown land; it is a forgotten land, and our relation to God is a palimpsest rather than a tabula rasa. There is no one who has no faith. Every one of us stood at the foot of Sinai and beheld the voice that proclaimed, I am the Lord thy God.

Afterthought

In asserting: God exists, we merely bring down over-powering reality to the level of thought. Our belief is but an afterthought.

The transition from obliviousness to an awareness of God, is not a leap over a missing link in a syllogism but a retreat, giving up premises rather than adding one.

Faith Is a Blush

God
is unwilling to be alone,
and man
cannot forever remain impervious
to what He longs to show.
Those of us who cannot keep their striving back
find themselves at times
within the sight of the unseen
and become aglow with its rays
Some of us blush,
    others wear a mask.
Faith is a blush
in the presence of God.

The Right of Interpretation

We must beware lest we violate the holy,
lest our dogmas overthink the mystery,
lest our psalms sing it away.

The right of interpretation
is given only to one who covers his face,
"afraid to look at God,"
to one who, when the vision is forced upon him,
says:
"I am undone . . .
for mine eyes have seen the King."
We can only drink the flow of thoughts
out of the rock of their words.

Metaphors

Only words that would not be trite in the presence
    of a dying man,
only ideas that would not pale in the face of the rising sun
or in the midst of a violent earthquake:
"God is One"
or:
"Holy, Holy, Holy is the Lord of Hosts . . ."
may be used as metaphors
in speaking of God.

Light

God is not a hypothesis derived from logical assumptions,
but an immediate insight, self-evident as light. He is not
something to be sought in the darkness with the light of
reason.

He *is* the light.

6

Ineffable

To meditative minds the ineffable is cryptic, inarticulate: dots, marks of secret meaning, scattered hints, to be gathered, deciphered and formed into evidence; while in moments of insight the ineffable is a metaphor in a forgotten mother tongue.

By Degrees

. . . Awareness of God does not come by degrees
from timidity to intellectual temerity;
it is not a decision reached at the crossroads of doubt.
It comes when, drifting in the wilderness,
    having gone astray,
we suddenly behold the immutable polar star.
Out of endless anxiety,
out of denial and despair,
the soul bursts out in speechless crying.

Light in the Cage

The world in which we live is a vast cage within a maze, high as our mind, wide as our power of will, long as our life span. Those who have never reached the rails or seen what is beyond the cage know of no freedom to dream of and are willing to rise and fight for civilizations that come and go and sink into the abyss of oblivion, an abyss which they never fill.

In our technological age man could not conceive of this world as anything but material for his own fulfillment. He considered himself the sovereign of his destiny, capable of organizing the breeding of races, of adapting a philosophy to his transient needs and of creating a religion at will. He postulated the existence of a Power that would serve as a guarantee for his self-fulfillment, as if God were a henchman to cater to man's aspirations and help him draw the utmost out of life.

But even those who have knocked their heads against the rails of the cage and discovered that life is involved in conflicts which they cannot solve; that the drive of possessiveness, which fills streets, homes and hearts with its clamor and shrill, is constantly muffled by the irony of time; that our constructiveness is staved in by self-destructiveness—even they prefer to live on the sumptuous, dainty diet within the cage rather than look for an exit to the maze in order to search for freedom in the darkness of the undisclosed.

Others, however, who cannot stand it, despair. They have no power to spend on faith any more, no goal to strive for, no strength to seek a goal. But, then, a moment comes like a thunderbolt, in which a flash of the undisclosed rends our dark apathy asunder. It is full of overpowering brilliance, like a point in which all moments of life are focused or a thought which outweighs all thoughts ever conceived of. There is so much light in our cage, in our world, it is as if it were suspended amidst the stars. Apathy turns to splendor unawares. The ineffable has shuddered itself into the soul. It has entered our consciousness like a ray of light passing into a lake. Refraction of that penetrating ray brings about a turning in our mind: We are penetrated by His insight. We cannot think any more as if He were there and we here. He is both there and here. He is not *a being*, but *being in and beyond all beings*.

A tremor seizes our limbs; our nerves are struck, quiver like strings; our whole being bursts into shudders. But then a cry, wrested from our very core, fills the world around us, as if a mountain were suddenly about to place itself in front of us. It is one word: GOD. Not an emotion, a stir within us, but a power, a marvel beyond us, tearing the world apart. The word that means more than universe, more than eternity, holy, holy, holy; we cannot comprehend it. We only know it means infinitely more than we are able to echo. Staggered, embarrassed, we stammer and say: He, who is more than all there is, who speaks through the ineffable, whose question is more than our mind can answer; He to whom our life can be the spelling of an answer.

An inspiration passes, having been inspired never passes. It remains like an island across the restlessness of time, to which we move over the wake of undying wonder. An eagerness is left behind, a craving and a feeling of shame at our ever being tainted with oblivion. . . .

We may be able to say no, if we decide to feed our mind on presumption and conceit, to cling to duplicity and to refuse to mean what we sense, to think what we feel. But there is no man who is not shaken for an instant by the eternal. And if we claim we have no heart to feel, no soul to hear, let us pray for tears or a feeling of shame.

Syntax of Silence

Our awareness of God is a syntax of the silence in which our souls mingle with the divine, in which the ineffable in us communes with the ineffable beyond us.

It is the afterglow of years in which soul and sky are silent together, the outgrowth of accumulated certainty of the abundant, never-ebbing presence of the divine.

All we ought to do is to let the insight be and to listen to the soul's recessed certainty of its being a parenthesis in the immense script of God's eternal speech.

Sharers of Gentle Joy

Mindfulness of God rises slowly, a thought at a time. Suddenly we are there. Or is He here, at the margin of our soul? When we begin to feel a qualm of diffidence lest we hurt what is holy, lest we break what is whole, then we discover that He is not austere. He answers with love our trembling awe.

Repentant of forgetting Him even for a while, we become sharers of gentle joy; we would like to dedicate ourselves forever to the unfoldment of His final order.

Starving for God

Some men go on a hunger strike in the prison of the mind, starving for God. There is joy, ancient and sudden, in this starving. There is reward, a grasp of the intangible, in the flaming reverie breaking through the bars of thought.

An Eternal Flutter

He who is satisfied has never truly craved,
and he who craves for the light of God
neglects his ease for ardor,

his life for love,
knowing that contentment is the shadow
not the light.
The great yearning that sweeps eternity
is a yearning to praise,
    a yearning to serve.
And when the waves of that yearning swell in our souls
all the barriers are pushed aside:
the crust of callousness,
    the hysteria of vanity,
        the orgies of arrogance.
For it is not the I that trembles alone,
it is not a stir out of my soul
but an eternal flutter that sweeps us all.

The Whole Wheat of Spirit

To the pious man God is as real as life, and as nobody
would be satisfied with mere knowing or reading about life,
so he is not content to suppose or to prove logically that there
is a God; he wants to feel and to give himself to Him; not
only to obey but to approach Him. His desire is to taste the
whole wheat of spirit before it is ground by the millstone of
reason. He would rather be overwhelmed by the symbols of
the inconceivable than wield the definitions of the superficial.

Stirred by a yearning after the unattainable, a pious man
is not content with being confined to what he is. His desire
is not only to *know* more than what ordinary reason has to
offer, but to *be* more than what he is; to transform the soul
into a vessel for the transcendent, to grasp with the sense

what is hidden from the mind, to express in symbols what the tongue cannot speak and what the reason cannot conceive, to experience as reality what vaguely dawns in intuitions.

God and the World

God and the world are not opposite poles. There is darkness in the world, but there is also this call, "Let there be light!" Nor are body and soul at loggerheads. We are not told to decide "Either-Or," either God or the world, either this world or the world to come. We are told to accept Either *and* Or, God *and* the world. It is upon us to strive for a share in the world to come, as well as to let God have a share in this world.

Waiting

God is not hiding in a temple. The Torah came to tell inattentive man: "You are not alone, you live constantly in a holy neighborhood; remember: 'Love thy neighbor—God—as thyself' " We are not asked to abandon life and to say farewell to this world, but to keep the spark within aflame, and to suffer His light to reflect in our face. Let our greed not rise like a barrier to this neighborhood.

God is waiting on every road that leads from intention to action, from desire to satisfaction.

God Desires

For thousands of years the deity and darkness were thought to be the same: a being, self-attached and full of blind desires; a being whom man revered but did not trust; that would reveal itself to the mad but not to the meek. For thousands of years it was accepted as a fact that the ultimate deity was hostile to man and could only be appeased by offerings of blood, until the prophets came who could not bear to see the defeat of God at the hands of fear, and proclaimed that darkness was His abode, not His essence; that as bright as midday's sun was His voice, giving an answer to the question: What does God desire?

Is it music?

> Take away from me the noise of your songs
> And to the melody of your lyres I will not listen.
> (Amos 5:23)

Is it prayer?

> When you spread out your hands,
>   I will hide my eyes from you;
> Though you make many a prayer,
>   I will not listen;
> Your hands are full of bloodshed.
> (Isaiah 1:15–16)

Is it sacrifice?

> Does the Lord delight in burnt offerings
>   and sacrifices
> as much as in obedience to the voice of
>   the Lord?
> (I Samuel 15:22)

And now, O Israel, what does the Lord your God require of you but to stand in awe of the Lord your God, walk in His ways, love Him, serve the Lord your God with all your mind and heart, and keep the commands of the

Lord and His statutes that I am commanding you today, for your good?

(Deuteronomy 10:12)

All Concern

The God of the philosophers is all indifference, too sublime to possess a heart or to cast a glance at our world. His wisdom consists in being conscious of Himself and oblivious to the world.

In contrast, the God of the prophets is all concern, too merciful to remain aloof to His creation. He not only rules the world in the majesty of His might; He is personally concerned and even stirred by the conduct and fate of man.

"His mercy is upon all His works." (Psalms 145:9).

At One

Unity of God
is power for unity of God with all things.
He is one in Himself
and striving to be one with the world.

Church and God

We worry a great deal about the problem of church and state. Now what about the church and God?

Sometimes there seems to be a greater separation between the church and God than between the church and state.

An Earnest

The man who lives by his faith is he who—even if scholars the world over should proclaim, if all mankind by an overwhelming majority of votes should endorse and if experiments . . . should corroborate that there is no God—would rather suffer at the hands of reason than accept his own reason as an idol; who would grieve, but neither totter nor betray the dignity of his sense of inadequacy in the presence of the ineffable.

For faith is an earnest we hold till the hour of passing away, not to be redeemed by a doctrine or even exchanged for insights.

What God means is expressed in the words: "For Thy kindness is better than life" (Psalms 63:4).

Like a Bell

Faith is not the clinging to a shrine but an endless pilgrimage of the heart. Audacious longing, burning songs, daring thoughts, an impulse overwhelming the heart, usurping the mind—these are all a drive towards serving Him who rings our hearts like a bell. It is as if He were waiting to enter our empty, perishing lives.

Faith

Faith is not a feature of man's mentality: self-effacement of curiosity, asceticism of reason, some psychic quality that has bearing on man alone. Its essence is not disclosed in the way we utter it, but in the soul's being in accord with what is relevant to God; in the extension of our love to what God may approve, our being carried away by the tide of His thoughts, rising beyond the desolate ken of man's despair.

Reciprocal

Faith is real only when it is not one-sided but reciprocal. Man can rely on God, if God can rely on man. To have faith means to justify God's faith in man. Faith is awareness of divine mutuality and companionship, a form of communion between God and man.

The Holy Dimension

What gives rise to faith is not a sentiment, a state of mind, an aspiration, but an everlasting fact in the universe, something which is prior to and independent of human knowledge and experience—*the holy dimension* of all existence. The objective side of religion is the spiritual constitution of the universe, the divine values invested in every being and exposed to the mind and will of man; an ontological relation. This is why the objective or the divine side of religion eludes psychological and sociological analysis.

All actions are not only agencies in the endless series of cause and effect; they also affect and concern God, with or without human consent. All existence stands in the dimension of the holy and nothing can be conceived of as living outside of it. All existence stands before God—here, everywhere, now and at all times. Not only a vow or conversion, not only the focusing of the mind upon God, engages man to

Him; all deeds, thoughts, feelings and events are His concern.

Just as man lives in the realm of nature and is subject to its laws, so does he find himself in the holy dimension. He can escape its bounds as little as he can take leave of nature. He can sever himself from the dimension of the holy neither by sin nor by stupidity, neither by apostasy nor by ignorance. There is no escape from God.

To have faith is consciously to enter a dimension in which we abide by our very existence. Piety is a response, the subjective corelative of an objective condition, the awareness of living within the holy dimension.

Lifting the Veil

God is not always silent, and man is not always blind. In every man's life there are moments when there is a lifting of the veil at the horizon of the known, opening a sight of the eternal. Each of us has at least once in his life experienced the momentous reality of God. Each of us has once caught a glimpse of the beauty, peace and power that flow through the souls of those who are devoted to Him. But such experiences are rare events. To some people they are like shooting stars, passing and unremembered. In others they kindle a light that is never quenched. The remembrance of that experience and the loyalty to the response of that moment are the forces that sustain our faith. In this sense, *faith is faithfulness*, loyalty to an event, loyalty to our response.

Embarrassment

Faith in the living God is not easily attained. Had it been possible to prove His existence beyond dispute, atheism would have been refuted as an error long ago. Had it been possible to awaken in every man the power to answer His ultimate question, the great prophets would have achieved it long ago.

Tragic is the embarrassment of the man of faith. "My tears have been my food day and night, while they say unto me all the day, where is thy God?" (Psalms 42:4). "Where are all His marvelous works which our father told us of?" (Nehemiah 6:13; see Psalms 44:2). "How long, O Lord, wilt Thou hide Thyself perpetually?" (Psalms 89:47). "My God, my God, why has Thou forsaken me?" (Psalms 22:2).

Why, we often ask in our prayers, hast Thou made it so difficult to find Thee? Why must we encounter so much anguish and travail before we can catch a glance of Thy presence? What a sad spectacle are the honest efforts of the great minds to prove Thy existence! And why dost Thou permit faith to blend so easily with bigotry, arrogance, cruelty, folly and superstition?

> O Lord, why dost Thou make us err from Thy ways
> And harden our heart, so that we fear Thee not?
> (Isaiah 63:17)

Signposts and Testimonies

We cannot make Him visible to us, but we can make ourselves visible to Him. So we open our thoughts to Him—feeble our tongues, but sensitive our hearts. We see more than we can say. The trees stand like guards of the Everlasting; the flowers like signposts of His goodness—only *we* have failed to be testimonies to His presence, tokens of His trust.

How could we have lived in the shadow of greatness and defied it?

A Cup in God's Hand

The pious man is possessed by his awareness of the presence and nearness of God. Everywhere and at all times he lives as in His sight, whether he remains always heedful of His proximity or not. He feels embraced by God's mercy as by a vast encircling space. Awareness of God is as close to him as the throbbing of his own heart, often deep and calm but at times overwhelming, intoxicating, setting the soul afire. The momentous reality of God stands there as peace, power and endless tranquility, as an inexhaustible source of help, as boundless compassion, as an open gate awaiting prayer.

It sometimes happens that the life of a pious man becomes so involved in God that his heart overflows as though it were a cup in the hand of God.

Dogmas

Are dogmas unnecessary?

We cannot be in rapport with the reality of the divine except for rare, fugitive moments. How can those moments be saved for the long hours of functional living, when the thoughts that feed like bees on the inscrutable desert us and we lose the sight and the drive?

Dogmas are like amber in which bees, once alive, are embalmed, and are capable of being electrified when our minds become exposed to the power of the ineffable.

PRAYER

The Light of God

Worship
is a way of seeing the world
in the light of God.

In the Mirror of the Holy

We do not step out of the world when we pray; we merely see the world in a different setting. The self is not the hub, but the spoke of the revolving wheel. In prayer we shift the center of living from self-consciousness to self-surrender. God is the center toward which all forces tend. He is the source, and we are the flowing of His force, the ebb and flow of His tides.

Prayer takes the mind out of the narrowness of self-interest, and enables us to see the world in the mirror of the holy. For when we betake ourselves to the extreme opposite of the ego, we can behold a situation from the aspect of God.

At the Border

Prayer is arrival at the border.
The dominion is Thine.

Take away from me
all that may not enter Thy realm.

Worth Saving

Prayer may not save us,
but prayer makes us worth saving.

God Listens

Dark is the world for me
for all its cities and stars.
If not for the certainty that God listens
                              to our cry,
who could stand so much misery,
so much callousness?

Surrendering to Stillness

We do not refuse to pray; we abstain from it. We ring the
hollow bell of selfishness rather than absorb the stillness that
surrounds the world, hovering over all the restlessness and
fear of life—the secret stillness that precedes our birth and
succeeds our death. Futile self-indulgence brings us out of
tune with the gentle song of nature's waiting, of mankind's
striving for salvation.

Is not listening to the pulse of wonder worth silence and
abstinence from self-asserting? Why do we not set apart an
hour of living for devotion to God by surrendering to stillness?

We dwell on the edge of mystery and ignore it, wasting
our souls, risking our stake in God. We constantly pour our

inner light away from Him, setting up the thick screen of self between Him and us, adding more shadows to the darkness that already hovers between Him and our wayward reason. Accepting surmises as dogmas, and prejudices as solutions, we ridicule the evidence of life for what is more than life. Our mind has ceased to be sensitive to the wonder. . . .

Rushing through the ecstasies of ambition, we only awake when plunged into dread or grief. In darkness, then, we grope for solace, for meaning, for prayer.

Gratefulness

To pray is to regain a sense of the mystery that animates all beings, the divine margin in all attainments. Prayer is our humble answer to the inconceivable surprise of living. It is all we can offer in return for the mystery by which we live. Who is worthy to be present at the constant unfolding of time? Amidst the meditation of mountains, the humility of flowers—wiser than all alphabets—clouds that die constantly for the sake of His glory, we are hating, hunting, hurting. Suddenly we feel ashamed of our clashes and complaints in the face of the tacit glory in nature. It is so embarrassing to live! How strange we are in the world, and how presumptuous our doings! Only one response can maintain us: gratefulness for witnessing the wonder, for the gift of our unearned right to serve, to adore, and to fulfill. It is gratefulness which makes the soul great.

God

The issue of prayer is not prayer;
the issue of prayer is God.

Exile

The true motivation for prayer is not, as it has been said, the sense of being at home in the universe, but rather the sense of not being at home in the universe.

Is there a sensitive heart that could stand indifferent and feel at home in the sight of so much evil and suffering, in the face of countless failures to live up to the will of God? On the contrary, the experience of not being at home in the world is a motivation for prayer.

That experience gains intensity in the amazing awareness that God himself is not at home in the universe. He is not at home in a universe where His will is defied and where His kingship is denied. God is in exile; the world is corrupt. The universe itself is not at home.

To pray means to bring God back into the world, to establish His kingship for a second at least. To pray means to expand His presence.

Attachment to the Utmost

As a tree torn form the soil, as a river separated from its source, the human soul wanes when detached from what is greater than itself. Without the holy, the good turns chaotic; without the good, beauty becomes accidental. It is the pattern of the impeccable which makes the average possible. It is the attachment to what is spiritually superior: loyalty to a sacred person or idea, devotion to a noble friend or teacher, love for a people or for mankind, which holds our inner life together. But any ideal, human, social, or artistic, if it forms a roof over all of life, shuts us off from the light. Even the palm of one hand may bar the light of the entire sun. Indeed, we must be open to the remote in order to perceive the near. Unless we aspire to the utmost, we shrink to inferiority.

Prayer is our attachment to the utmost. Without God in sight, we are like the scattered rungs of a broken ladder. To pray is to become a ladder on which thoughts mount to God to join the movement toward Him which surges unnoticed throughout the entire universe.

To Discern

Prayer is a way to master what is inferior in us, to discern between the signal and the trivial, between the vital and the futile, by taking counsel with what we know about the will of God, by seeing our fate in proportion to God.

Quarantine for the Soul

Prayer clarifies our hopes and intentions. It helps us discover our true aspirations, the pangs we ignore, the longings we forget. It is an act of self-purification, a quarantine for the soul. It gives us the opportunity to be honest, to say what we believe, and to stand for what we say. For the accord of assertion and conviction, thought and conscience is the basis of all prayer.

What to Aspire to

Prayer teaches us what to aspire to.

So often we do not know what to cling to. Prayer implants in us the ideals we ought to cherish. Redemption, purity of mind and tongue, or willingness to help, may hover as ideas before our mind, but the idea becomes a concern, something to long for, a goal to be reached, when we pray:

> Guard my tongue from evil
> and my lips from speaking guile;
> and in the face of those who curse me,
> let my soul be silent.

The Gulf Stream

On the globe of the microcosm the flow of prayer is like the Gulf Stream, imparting warmth to all that is cold, melting all that is hard in our life. For even loyalties may freeze to indifference if detached from the stream which carries the strength to be loyal. How often does justice lapse into cruelty, and righteousness into hypocrisy. Prayer revives and keeps alive the rare greatness of some past experience in which things glowed with meaning and blessing. It remains important, even when we ignore it for a while, like a candlestick set aside for the day. Night will come, and we shall again gather round its tiny flame. Our affection for the trifles of living will be mixed with longing for the comfort of all men.

No Panacea

However, prayer is no panacea, no substitute for action. It is, rather, like a beam thrown from a flashlight before us into the darkness. It is in this light that we who grope, stumble, and climb, discover where we stand, what surrounds us, and the course which we should choose. Prayer makes visible the right, and reveals what is hampering and false. In its radiance, we behold the worth of our efforts, the range of our hopes, and the meaning of our deeds.

Witness the Wonder

The idea of prayer may seem to be the assumption of man's ability to accost God, to lay our hopes, sorrows, and wishes before Him. But this assumption is a paraphrase, rather than a precise expression of what we believe. We do not feel that we possess a magic power of speaking to the Infinite; we merely witness the wonder of prayer, the wonder of man addressing himself to the Eternal. Contact with Him is not our achievement. It is a gift, coming down to us from on high like a meteor, rather than rising up like a rocket. Before the words of prayer come to the lips, the mind must believe in God's willingness to draw near to us, and in our ability to clear the path for His approach. Such belief is the idea that leads us toward prayer.

Shame and Joy

Prayer is like the light from a burning glass in which all the rays that emanate from the soul are gathered to a focus. There are hours when we are resplendent with the glowing awareness of our share in His secret interests on earth. We pray. We are carried forward to Him who is coming close to us. We endeavor to divine His will, not merely His command. Prayer is an answer to God: "Here am I. And this is the record of my days. Look into my heart, into my hopes and my regrets." We depart in shame and joy.

Yet prayer never ends, for faith endows us with a bold craving that He draw near to us and approach us as a father— not only as a ruler; not only through our walking in His ways, but through His entering into our ways.

A Thought of God

The purpose of prayer is to be brought to His attention, to be listened to, to be understood by Him; not to know Him, but to *be known* to Him. To pray is to behold life not only as a result of His power, but as a concern of His will, or to strive to make our life a divine concern. For the ultimate aspiration of man is not to be a master, but an object of His knowledge. To live "in the light of His countenance," to become a thought of God—this is the true career of man.

Not the Self

The focus of prayer is not the self. . . . It is the momentary disregard of our personal concerns, the absence of self-centered thoughts, which constitute the art of prayer. . . . Thus, in beseeching Him for bread, there is *one* instant, at least, in which our mind is directed neither to our hunger nor to food, but to His mercy. This instant is prayer.

We start with a personal concern and live to feel the utmost.

An Invitation

Prayer is an invitation to God to intervene in our lives, to let His will prevail in our affairs; it is the opening of a window to Him in our will, an effort to make Him the Lord of our soul. We submit our interests to His concern, and seek to be allied with what is ultimately right. Our approach to the holy is not an intrusion, but an answer. Between the dawn of childhood and the door of death, man encounters things and events out of which comes a whisper of truth, not much louder than stillness, but exhorting and persistent. Yet man listens to his fears and his whims, rather than to the gentle petitions of God. The Lord of the universe is suing for the favor of man.

His Affair

Prayer is spiritual ecstasy.

It is as if all our vital thoughts in fierce ardor would burst the mind to stream toward God. A keen single force draws our yearning for the utmost out of the seclusion of the soul. We try to see our visions in His light, to feel our life as His affair.

We begin by letting the thought of Him engage our minds, by realizing His name and entering into a reverie which leads through beauty and stillness, from feeling to thought, and from understanding to devotion. For the coins of prayer bear the image of God's dreams and wishes for fear-haunted man.

Dreaming for God

At the beginning of all action is an inner vision in which things to be are experienced as real. Prayer, too, is frequently an inner vision, an intense dreaming for God—the reflection of the Divine intentions in the soul of man. We dream of a time "when the world will be perfected under the Kingship of God, and all the children of flesh will call upon Thy name, when Thou wilt turn unto Thyself all the wicked of the earth." We anticipate the fulfillment of the hope shared by both God and man.

To pray is to dream in league with God, to envision His holy visions.

The Lightness of a Dream

God is not alone when discarded by man.
But man is alone.
To avoid prayer constantly
is to force a gap between man and God
　　which can widen into an abyss.
But sometimes,
awakening on the edge of despair to weep,
　　and arising from forgetfulness,
we feel how yearning moves in softly
to become the lord of a restless breast,
and we pass over the gap
with the lightness of a dream.

Words

It takes two things to make prayer come to pass: a person and a word.

What do most of us know about the substance of words? Estranged from the soil of the soul, our words do not grow as fruits of insights, but are found as sapless clichés, refuse in the backyard of intelligence. To the man of our age nothing is as familiar and nothing as trite as words. . . . We all live in them, feel in them, think in them, but failing to uphold their independent dignity, to respect their power and weight, they turn waif, elusive—a mouthful of dust. . . .

Words have ceased to be commitments.

The Word of Prayer

Words of prayer are commitments,
We stand for what we utter. . . .
The word of prayer is like a pledge in the
    making.

To Confront the Word

It is not enough to articulate a sound. Unless one understands that the word is stronger than the will; unless one knows how to approach a word with all the joy, the hope or the grief he owns, prayer will hardly come to pass. The words must not fall off our lips like dead leaves in the autumn. They must rise like birds out of the heart into the vast expanse of eternity.

To begin to pray is to confront the word, to face its dignity, its singularity, and to sense its potential might. And it is the spiritual power of the praying man that makes manifest what is dormant in the text.

From Word to Word

An island in this world are the words of prayer. Each time when arriving at the shore, we face the same hazards, the same strain, tension and risk. Each time the island must be conquered, as if we had never been there before, as if we were strangers to the spirit. Rugged is the shore, and in the sight of majestic utterances we stand, seeking a kindred word on which to gain a foothold for our souls. The words we face are lofty, and the humble ones are concealed, beyond our reach. We must not be shaken. We must learn how to crawl, if we do not know how to leap. Prayer . . . does not complete itself in an instant, nor does it move on a level plane, but thrusts itself forward through depths and heights, through detours and byways. It runs its course as a gradually advancing action, from word to word, from thought to thought, from feeling to feeling. Arriving, we discover a level where words are treasures, where meanings lie hidden still to be mined. Restrained insights, slumbering emotions, the subdued voice of deeper knowledge bursts upon the mind.

We often discover that the word is greater than the mind. What we feel is so much less than what we say.

One Word

To pray
is to know how to stand still
and to dwell upon a word.

Beyond Words

Genuine prayer is an event in which man surpasses himself. Man hardly comprehends what is coming to pass. Its beginning lies on this side of the word, but the end lies beyond all words. What is happening is not always brought about by the power of man. At times all we do is to utter a word with all our heart, yet it is as if we lifted up a whole world. It is as if someone unsuspectingly pressed a button and a gigantic wheel-work were stormily and surprisingly set in motion.

Where Expression Ends

Prayer begins where expression ends. The words that reach our lips are often but waves of an overflowing stream touching the shore. We often seek and miss, struggle and fail to adjust our unique feelings to the patterns of texts. Where is the tree that can utter fully the silent passion of the soil? Words can only open the door, and we can only weep on the threshold of our incommunicable thirst after the incomprehensible.

Song

In no other act does man experience so often the disparity between the desire for expression and the means of expression as in prayer. The inadequacy of the means at our disposal appears so tangible, so tragic, that one feels it a grace to be able to give oneself up to music, to a tone, to a song, to a chant. The wave of a song carries the soul to heights which utterable meanings can never reach. Such abandonment is no escape. . . . For the world of unutterable meanings is the nursery of the soul, the cradle of all our ideas. It is not an escape but a return to one's origins.

A Crucible

The passage of hours is either an invitation to despair or a ladder to eternity. This little time in our hands melts away ere it can be formed. Before our eyes man and maid, spring and splendor, slide into oblivion. However, there are hours that perish and hours that join the everlasting. Prayer is a crucible in which time is cast in the likeness of the eternal. Man hands over his time to God in the secrecy of single words. When anointed by prayer, his thoughts and deeds do not sink into nothingness, but merge into the endless knowledge of an all-embracing God. We yield our thoughts to Him who endowed us with a chain of days for the duration of life.

SABBATH

The Seed of Eternity

He who wants to enter the holiness of the day must first lay down the profanity of clattering commerce, of being yoked to toil. He must go away from the screech of dissonant days, from the nervousness and fury of acquisitiveness and the betrayal in embezzling his own life. He must say farewell to manual work and learn to understand that the world has already been created and will survive without the help of man.

Six days a week we wrestle with the world, wringing profit from the earth; on the Sabbath we especially care for the seed of eternity planted in the soul. The world has our hands, but our soul belongs to Someone Else.

Six days a week we seek to dominate the world, on the seventh day we try to dominate the self.

Freedom

To set apart one day a week for freedom, a day on which we would not use the instruments which have been so easily turned into weapons of destruction, a day for being with ourselves, a day of detachment from the vulgar, of independence of external obligations, a day on which we stop worshipping the idols of technical civilization, a day of armistice in the economic struggle with our fellow men and the forces of nature—is there any institution that holds out a greater hope for man's progress than the Sabbath?

Peace

The seventh day is the armistice in man's cruel struggle for existence, a truce in all conflicts, personal and social, peace between man and man, man and nature, peace within man; a day on which handling money is considered a desecration, on which man avows his independence of that which is the world's chief idol.

The seventh day is the exodus from tension, the liberation of man from his own muddiness, the installation of man as a sovereign in the world of time.

Island of Stillness

In the tempestuous ocean of time and toil there are islands of stillness where man may enter a harbor and reclaim his dignity.

The island is the seventh day, the Sabbath, a day of detachment from things, instruments and practical affairs as well as of attachment to the spirit.

Architecture of Time

Jewish ritual may be characterized as the art of significant forms in time, as *architecture of time*. Most of its observances—the Sabbath, the New Moon, the festivals, the Sabbatical and the Jubilee year—depend on a certain hour of the day or season of the year. It is, for example, the evening, morning, or afternoon that brings with it the call to prayer. The main themes of faith lie in the realm of time. We remember the day of the exodus from Egypt, the day when Israel stood at Sinai; and our Messianic hope is the expectation of a day, of the end of days.

Holiness in Time

The meaning of the Sabbath is to celebrate time rather than space. Six days a week we live under the tyranny of things of space; on the Sabbath we try to become attuned to *holiness in time*. It is a day on which we are called upon to share in what is eternal in time, to turn from the results of creation to the mystery of creation; from the world of creation to the creation of the world.

The Great Cathedral

Judaism teaches us to be attached to holiness in time, to be attached to sacred events, to learn how to consecrate sanctuaries that emerge from the magnificent stream of a year.

The Sabbaths are our great cathedrals; and our Holy of

Holies is a shrine that neither the Romans nor the Germans were able to burn; a shrine that even apostasy cannot easily obliterate: the Day of Atonement.

A Palace in Time

The seventh day is a *palace in time* which we build. It is made of soul, of joy and reticence. In its atmosphere, a discipline is a reminder of adjacency to eternity. Indeed, the splendor of the day is expressed in terms of *abstentions*, just as the mystery of God is more adequately conveyed *via negationis*, in the categories of *negative theology* which claims that we can never say what He is, we can only say what He is not. We often feel how poor the edifice would be were it built exclusively of our rituals and deeds which are so awkward and often so obtrusive. How else express glory in the presence of eternity, if not by the silence of abstaining from noisy acts? These restrictions utter songs to those who know how to stay at a palace with a queen.

RELIGION

Something Asked

The beginning of faith is not a feeling for the mystery of living or a sense of awe, wonder and amazement. The root of religion is the question what to do with the feeling for the mystery of living, what to do with awe, wonder and amazement.

Religion begins with a consciousness that something is asked of us.

It is in that tense, eternal asking in which the soul is caught and in which man's answer is elicited.

Question and Answer

Religion consists of
God's question
and man's answer.

Religion

Religion is not
"what man does with his solitariness."
Religion is
what man does with the presence of God.

38

Ministers or Slaves

Mankind does not have the choice of religion and neutrality.

Irreligion is not opiate but poison. Our energies are too abundant for living indifferently. We are in need of an endless purpose to absorb our immense power, if our souls are not to run amok. We are either the ministers of the sacred or slaves of evil.

Religion

Little does contemporary religion ask of man.

It is ready to offer comfort; it has no courage to challenge. It is ready to offer edification; it has no courage to break the idols, to shatter callousness.

The trouble is that religion has become "religion"—institution, dogma, ritual. It is no longer an event. Its acceptance involves neither risk nor strain. Religion has achieved respectability by the grace of society, and its representatives publish as a frontispiece the *nihil obstat* signed by social scientists.

We define self-reliance and call it faith, shrewdness and call it wisdom, anthropology and call it ethics, literature and call it Bible, inner security and call it religion, conscience and call it God. However, nothing counterfeit can endure forever.

It is customary to blame secular science and antireligious philosophy for the eclipse of religion in modern society. It would be more honest to blame religion for its own defeats. Religion declined not because it was refuted, but because it became irrelevant, dull, oppressive, insipid.

When faith is completely replaced by creed, worship by

discipline, love by habit; when the crisis of today is ignored because of the splendor of the past; when faith becomes an heirloom rather than a living fountain; when religion speaks only in the name of authority rather than with the voice of compassion, its message becomes meaningless.

Not for Religion's Sake

It is an inherent weakness of religion not to take offense at the segregation of God, to forget that the true sanctuary has no walls. Religion has often suffered from the tendency to become parochial, self-indulgent, self-seeking; as if the task were not to ennoble human nature but to enhance the power and beauty of its institutions or to enlarge the body of doctrines. It has often done more to canonize prejudices than to wrestle for truth; to petrify the sacred than to sanctify the secular. Yet the task of religion is to be a challenge to the stabilization of values.

Religion is not for religion's sake but for God's sake.

For God's Sake

Religion as an institution, the Temple as an ultimate end, or, in other words, religion for religion's sake, is idolatry.

The fact is that evil is integral to religion, not only to secularism. Parochial saintliness may be an evasion of duty, an accommodation to selfishness.

Religion is for God's sake.

The human side of religion, its creeds, rituals and instructions is a way rather than the goal. The goal is "to do justice, to love mercy and to walk humbly *with* thy God." When the human side of religion becomes the goal, injustice becomes a way.

Power and Majesty

Tragic is the role of religion in contemporary society. The world is waiting to hear the Voice, and those who are called upon to utter the word are confused and weak in faith.

"The voice of the Lord is powerful; the voice of the Lord is full of majesty" (Psalm 29:4).

Where it its power?

Where is its majesty?

What of the Night?

This is a time to cry out.

One is ashamed to be human. One is embarrassed to be called religious in the face of religion's failure to keep alive the image of God in the face of man. . . . We have imprisoned God in our temples and slogans, and now the word of God is dying on our lips.

There is darkness in the East, and smugness in the West.

What of the night?

What of the night?

MAN

I. THE HUMAN PREDICAMENT

Paradise

After having eaten the forbidden fruit, the Lord sent forth
man from Paradise, to till the ground from which he was
taken. But man, who is more subtle than any other creature
that God has made, what did he do? He undertook to build
a Paradise by his own might, and he is driving God from his
Paradise.

Divine Eclipse

We have witnessed in history how often a man, a group or
a nation, lost from the sight of God, acts and succeeds, strives
and achieves, but is given up by Him. They may stride from
one victory to another and yet they are done with and abandoned. . . . They may possess all glory and might, but their
life will be dismal. God has withdrawn from their life, even
while they are heaping wickedness upon cruelty and malice

upon evil. The dismissal of man . . . inaugurates eventual calamity.

They are left alone, neither molested by punishment nor assured by indication of help. The divine does not interfere with their actions nor intervene in their conscience. Having all in abundance save His blessing, they find their wealth a shell in which there is curse without mercy.

The Message

Man is a messenger
who forgot the message.

Sin

Man's sin is in his failure to live what he is.
Being the master of the earth,
man forgets that he is servant of God.

Embarrassing

How embarrassing for man
to be the greatest miracle on earth
and not to understand it!
How embarrassing for man
to live in the shadow of greatness
and to ignore it,
to be a contemporary of God

and not to sense it.
Religion depends upon what man does
with his ultimate embarrassment.

In the Skyscrapers

Surely God will always receive a surprise of a handful of fools—who do not fail. There will always remain a spiritual underground where a few brave minds continue to fight.

Yet our concern is not how to worship in the catacombs but rather how to remain human in the skyscrapers.

The Mountain

When Israel approached Sinai,
God lifted up the mountain
and held it over their heads,
saying:
"Either you accept the Torah
or be crushed beneath the mountain."
The mountain of history is over our heads again.
Shall we renew the covenant with God?

Faith in Man

The great problem in the life of man is whether to trust, to have faith in God. The great problem in the life of God is whether to trust, to have faith in man.

44

The central issue is not man's decision to extend formal recognition to God, to furnish God with a certificate that he exists, but the realization of our importance to God's design; not to prove that God is alive, but to prove that man is not dead; not to prove him, but to prove ourselves.

Martyrdom

According to Albert Camus, "There is only one really serious philosophical problem: and that is suicide." May I differ and suggest that there is only one really serious problem: and that is martyrdom.

Is there anything worth dying for?

We can only live the truth if we have the power to die for it. Suicide is escape from evil and surrender to absurdity. A martyr is a witness to the holy in spite of evil absurdity.

Nietzsche's formula for the greatness of a human being is *amor fati*. Jewish tradition would suggest as the formula for the greatness of man his capacity for *kiddush hashem*, readiness to die for the sake of God, for the sake of the Name.

Beyond Good Intentions

Helpless and incongruous is man with all his craving, with his tiny candles in the mist. Is it his will to be good that would heal the wounds of his soul, his fright and frustration? It is too obvious that his will is a door to a house divided against itself, that his good intentions, after enduring for a while, touch the mud of vanity, like the horizon of his life which some day will touch the grave. Is there anything beyond the horizon of our good intentions?

Man Is Not Alone, p. 199

II. HUMAN NATURE

Intruder

A person wakes up one day and maintains that he is a rooster. We do not know what he means, and assign him to an insane asylum.

But when a person wakes up one day and maintains that he is a human being, we also do not know what he means.

Assuming that the earth were endowed with psychic power, it would raise the question: Who is he—the strange intruder who clips my wings, who trims my gardens? He who cannot live without me and is not quite a part of me?

Sacred

What do I see when I see a man?

I see him first as one other specimen of the human species, then as a specific, particular individual who can be named or identified; but then he stands before me as the only entity in nature with which sanctity is associated. All other sacred objects in space are made holy by man. Human life is the only type of being we consider intrinsically sacred, the only type of being we regard as supremely valuable.

The particular individual may not be dear to me—in fact, I may even dislike him. But he is dear to someone else, to his mother, for example, although that, too, is not the reason for his eminence. For even if nobody cares for him, he still is a human being.

Unique

Looking upon myself from the perspective of society, I am an average person. Facing myself intimately, immediately, I regard myself as unique, as exceedingly precious, not to be exchanged for anything else.

No one will live my life for me, no one will think my thoughts for me or dream my dreams.

In the eyes of the world, I am an average man. But to my heart I am not an average man. To my heart I am of great moment. The challenge I face is how to actualize the quiet eminence of my being.

Somebody

It is through the awareness that I am not only an every-body, that I evolve as a . . . somebody, as a person, as something that cannot be repeated, for which there is no duplicate, no substitute.

It is in the awareness of my being somebody that freedom comes to pass.

A Face

A human being has not only a body but also a face. A face cannot be grafted or interchanged. A face is a message, a face speaks, often unbeknown to the person. Is not the human face a living mixture of mystery and meaning? We are all able to see it, and are all unable to describe it. Is it not a strange marvel that among so many hundreds of millions of faces, no two faces are alike? And that no face remains quite the same for more than one instant? The most exposed part of the body, it is the least describable, a synonym for an incarnation of uniqueness. Can we look at a face as if it were a commonplace?

A Name

Individual examples of any kind of being are nameless; but every individual human being claims a name. A human individual is not a mere specimen of his species. You distort him by disregarding his uniqueness.

No man is an average man.

A Surprise

Being human is a novelty not a mere repetition or extension of the past, an anticipation of things to come. Being human is a surprise, not a foregone conclusion. A person has a capacity to create events. Every person is a disclosure, an example of exclusiveness.

One thing that sets man apart from animals is a boundless, unpredictable capacity for the development of an inner universe. There is more potentiality in his soul than in any other being known to us. Look at the infant and try to imagine the multitude of events it is going to engender. One child named Johann Sebastian Bach was charged with power enough to hold generations of men in his spell. But is there any potentiality to acclaim or any surprise to expect in a calf or a colt? Indeed, the enigma of human being is not in what he is but in what he is able to be.

His Image

The second commandment implies more than the prohibition of images; it implies rejection of all visible symbols for God; not only images fashioned by man but also of "any manner of likeness, of any thing that is in heaven above, or that is in the earth beneath, or that is in the water under the earth."

And yet there is something in the world that the Bible does regard as a symbol of God. It is not a temple or a tree, it is not a statue or a star. The symbol of God is *man, every man*. God created man in His image, in His likeness.

Image and Dust

There are two ways in which the Bible speaks of the creation of man. In the first chapter of the Book of Genesis, which is devoted to the creation of the physical universe, man is described as having been created in the *image and likeness* of God.

In the second chapter, which tells us of the commandmentnot to eat of the fruit of the tree of knowledge, man is described as having been formed *out of the dust* of the earth.

Together, *image* and *dust* express the polarity of the nature of man.

Dust and Image

Man . . . is a duality
of mysterious grandeur and pompous aridity,
a vision of God and a mountain of dust.
It is because of his being dust
that his iniquities may be forgiven,
and it is because of his being an image
that his righteousness is expected.

The Parting of the Ways

All that exists obeys. Man alone occupies a unique status. As a natural being he obeys, as a human being he must frequently choose; confined in his existence, he is unrestrained in his will. His acts do not emanate from him like rays of energy from matter. Placed in the parting of the ways, he must time and again decide which direction to take. The course of his life is, accordingly, unpredictable; no one can write his autobiography in advance.

God or the Snake

Man is continuous both with the rest of organic nature and with the infinite outpouring of the spirit of God. A minority in the realm of being, he stands somewhere between God and the beasts. Unable to live alone, he must commune with either of the two.

Both Adam and the beasts were blessed by the Lord, but man was also charged with conquering the earth and dominating the beast. Man is always faced with the choice of listening either to God or to the snake. It is always easier to envy the beast . . . than to hearken to the Voice.

Seesawing

Our existence seesaws between animality and divinity, between that which is more and that which is less than humanity: below is evanescence, futility, and above is the open door of the divine exchequer where we lay up the sterling coin of piety and spirit, the immortal remains of our dying lives.

We are constantly in the mills of death, but we are also the contemporaries of God.

A Pendulum

Man is "a little lower than the angels" and a little higher than the beasts.

Like a pendulum he swings to and fro under the combined

action of gravity and momentum, of the gravitation of selfishness and the momentum of the divine, of a vision beheld by God in the darkness of flesh and blood.

Only in the Depths

We are prone to be impressed by the ostentatious, the obvious. The strident caterwaul of the animal fills the air, while the still small voice of the spirit is heard only in the rare hours of prayer and devotion. From the streetcar window we may see the hunt for wealth and pleasure, the onslaught upon the weak, faces expressing suspicion or contempt. On the other hand, the holy lives only in the depths. What is noble retires when exposed to light, humility is extinguished in the awareness of it, and the willingness for martyrdom rests in the secrecy of the things to be. Walking upon the clay, we live in nature, surrendering to impulse and passion, to vanity and arrogance, while our eyes reach out to the lasting light of truth. We are subject to terrestrial gravitation, yet we are confronted by God.

Wavering

If man is not more than human, then he is less than human.

Man is but a short, critical stage between the animal and the spiritual. His state is one of constant wavering, of soaring or descending. Undeviating humanity is nonexistent.

The emancipated man is yet to emerge.

Naked

There is hardly a person who does not submit his soul to the beauty parlor, who does not employ the make-up of vanity in order to belie his embarrassment.

It is only before God that we all stand naked.

Sacred

The universe is not a waif and life is not a derelict. Man is neither the lord of the universe nor even the master of his own destiny. Our life is not our own property but a possession of God. And it is this divine ownership that makes life a sacred thing.

The Knot

Man is more than what he is to himself. In his reason he may be limited, in his will he may be wicked, yet he stands in a relation to God which he may betray but not sever and which constitutes the essential meaning of life.

He is the knot in which heaven and earth are interlaced.

God's Dream

It is an accepted fact that the Bible has given the world a new concept of God. What is not realized is the fact that the Bible has given the world a new vision of man. The Bible is not a book about God; it is a book about man.

From the perspective of the Bible:
Who is man?

A being in travail with God's dreams, with God's dream of a world redeemed, of reconciliation of heaven and earth.

God's dream is not to be alone, to have mankind as a partner in the drama of continuous creation. By whatever we do . . . we either advance or obstruct the drama of redemption; we either reduce or enhance the power of evil.

A Need of God

Man is man because something divine is at stake in his existence. He is not an innocent bystander in the cosmic drama. There is in us more kinship with the divine than we are able to believe.

The souls of men are candles of the Lord, lit on the cosmic way, . . . and every soul is indispensable to Him.

Man is needed,
he is *a need of God.*

III. THE HUMAN TASK

A Divine Dream

There is a divine dream which the prophets and rabbis have cherished and which fills our prayers, and permeates the acts of true piety. It is the dream of a world, rid of evil by the grace of God as well as by the efforts of man, by his dedication to the task of establishing the kinship of God in the world. God is waiting for us to redeem the world. We should not spend our life hunting for trivial satisfactions while God is waiting.

God's Time

Living is not a private affair of the individual.
Living is what man does with God's time,
what man does with God's world.

Alone

It is as if I were the only man on the globe
and God, too, were alone,
waiting for me.

The Likeness of God

Verbally, we seem to be committed to the idea that man is created in the likeness of God. But are we committed to it intellectually?

If the divine likeness is our premise, then the question arises: How should a being created in the likeness of God act, think, feel? How should we live in a way which is compatible with our being a likeness of God?

55

To Stand For

To be
Is
To stand for

How?

How should I live the life that I am?

Unpolluted

While man is attached to the ultimate at the root of his being, he is detached and uncurbed in his thoughts and deeds, free to act and free to refrain; he has the power to disobey. Yet a tree is known by its fruits, not by its roots. There are no ugly trees but there are wormy fruits. Only one question, therefore, is worthy of supreme anxiety: How to live in a world pestered with lies and remain unpolluted, how not to be stricken with despair, not to flee but to fight and succeed in keeping the soul unsoiled and even aid in purifying the world?

Extreme Views

Throughout the ages two extreme views . . . have most frequently been voiced—one deifying desire, the other vili-fying it. There were those who, overwhelmed by the dark

56

power of passion, believed that they sensed in its raving a manifestation of the gods and celebrated its gratification as a sacred ritual. Dionysian orgies, fertility rites, sacred prostitution are extreme examples of a view that subconsciously has never died out.

The exponents of the other extreme, frightened by the destructive power of unbridled passion, have taught man to see ugliness in desire, Satan in the rapture of the flesh. Their advice was to repress the appetites, and their ideal, self-renunciation and asceticism. Some Greeks said: "Passion is a god, Eros"; Buddhists say: "Desire is evil."

To the Jewish mind, being neither enticed nor horrified by the powers of passion, desires are neither benign nor pernicious but, like fire, they do not agree with straw. They should be neither quenched nor supplied with fuel. Rather than worship fire and be consumed by it, we should let a light come out of the flames. Needs are spiritual opportunities.

Sacred

The road to the sacred leads through the secular.

No Neutrality

. . . The world is not a vacuum.
Either we make it an altar for God
or it is invaded by demons.
There can be no neutrality.
Either we are ministers of the sacred
or slaves of evil.

Not Beyond Our Will

We live by the conviction that acts of goodness
reflect the hidden light of His holiness.
His light is above our minds
but not beyond our will.
It is within our power to mirror His unending love
in deeds of kindness,
like brooks that hold the sky.

Between Good and Evil

The power to make distinctions is a primary operation of intelligence. We distinguish between white and black, beautiful and ugly, pleasant and unpleasant, gain and loss, good and evil, right and wrong.

The fate of mankind depends upon the realization that the distinction between good and evil, right and wrong, is superior to all other distinctions. . . . To teach humanity the primacy of that distinction is of essence to the Biblical message.

After the Lord had created the universe, He took a look at His creation. What was the word that conveyed His impression? If an artist were to find a word describing how the universe looked to God at the dawn of its existence, the word would be sublime or beautiful. But the word that the Bible has is *good*. Indeed, when looking through a telescope into the stellar space, the word that comes to our mind is grandeur, mystery, splendor. But the God of Israel is not impressed with splendor; He is impressed with goodness.

Good and evil are not values among other values. Good is life, and evil is death. "See I have set before thee this day life and good, death and evil . . . choose life" (Deuteronomy 30:15, 19).

The Grandeur of Living

How should man, a being created in the likeness of God, live? What way of living is compatible with the grandeur and mystery of life? It is a problem which man has always been anxious to ignore. Upon the pavement of the Roman city of Timgat an inscription was found which reads: "To hunt, to bathe, to gamble, to laugh, that is to live." Judaism is a reminder of the grandeur and earnestness of living.

In what dimension of existence does man become aware of the grandeur and earnestness of living? . . .

It is in *deeds* that man becomes aware of what his life really is, of his power to harm and to hurt, to wreck and to ruin; of his ability to derive joy and to bestow it upon others; to relieve and to increase his own and other people's tensions. It is in the employment of his will, not in reflection, that he meets his own self as it is; not as he should like it to be. In his deeds man exposes his immanent as well as his suppressed desires, spelling even that which he cannot apprehend. What he may not dare to think, he often utters in deeds. The heart is revealed in the deeds.

A Song of Deeds

Man can be a nightmare but also a fulfillment of a vision of God. He has been given the power to surpass himself; to answer for all things and to act for one God. All beings obey the law; man is able to sing the law. His ultimate legacy is in his composing a song of deeds which only God fully understands.

Great the Challenge

Great is the challenge we face at every moment
sublime the occasion, every occasion.
Here we are, contemporaries of God,
some of His power at our disposal.

Expectations

Over and above personal problems, there is an objective
challenge to overcome inequity, injustice, helplessness,
suffering, carelessness, oppression. Over and above the din
of desires there is a calling, a demanding, a waiting, an
expectation. There is a question that follows me wherever I
turn. What is expected of me? What is demanded of me?

What we encounter is not only flowers and stars, mountains and walls. Over and above all things is a sublime expectation, a waiting for. With every child born a new expectation
enters the world.

This is the most important experience in the life of every
human being: something is asked of me. Every human being
has had a moment in which he sensed a mysterious waiting
for him. Meaning is found in responding to the demand,
meaning is found in sensing the demand.

A Song Every Day

The meaning of existence is experienced in moments of
exaltation. Man must strive for the summit in order to survive
on the ground . . . his ends must surpass his needs. The
security of existence lies in the exaltation of existence.

60

This is one of the rewards of being human: quiet exaltation, capability for celebration. It is expressed in a phrase which Rabbi Akiba offered to his disciples:
A song every day,
A song every day.

What We Owe

The world was not made by man.
The earth is the Lord's,
not a derelict.
What we own, we owe.
"How shall I ever repay to the Lord
all his bounties to me!" (Psalm 116:12).

Parent

What is characteristic of the modern family is that on the level of profound personal experience, parents and children live apart. The experiences shared at home are perfunctory rather than creative. In the past, it was the role of the father to lead the children through moments of exaltation. Whatever stood out as venerable and lofty was associated with the father. Now we are entering a social structure in which the father is becoming obsolete, and in which there are only three ages: childhood, adolescence, and old age. The husband of the mother is not a father, he is a regular guy, a playmate for the boys, engaged in the same foibles and subject to similar impulses. Since he neither represents the legacy of the past nor is capable of keeping pace with the boys in the pursuit of the future, his status is rather precarious.

Children today experience their highest moments of exaltation in a children's world, in which there is no room for parents. But unless a fellowship of spiritual experience is re-established, the parent will remain an outsider to the child's soul. This is one of the beauties of the human spirit. We appreciate *what we share*, we do not appreciate *what we receive*. Friendship, affection is not acquired by giving presents. Friendship, affection comes about by two people sharing a significant moment, by having an experience in common.

The Parent

The Heart of the Ten Commandments is to be found in the words: *Revere thy father and thy mother*.

The problem I as a father face, is why my child should revere me.

Unless my child will sense in my personal existence acts and attitudes that evoke reverence—the ability to delay satisfactions, to overcome prejudices, to sense the holy to strive for the noble—why should he/she revere me?

Teacher

Everything depends on the person who stands in the front of the classroom. The teacher is not an automatic fountain from which intellectual beverages may be obtained. He is either a witness or a stranger. To guide a pupil into the promised land, he must have been there himself. When asking himself: Do I stand for what I teach? Do I believe what I say? he must be able to answer in the affirmative.

What we need more than anything else is not *textbooks* but *textpeople*. It is the personality of the teacher which is the text that the pupils read; the text that they will never forget.

Youth

"What message have you for young people?" asked Carl Stern of NBC in concluding a television interview with Rabbi Abraham Joshua Heschel shortly before his death.

Rabbi Heschel replied: ". . . Let them remember that there is a meaning beyond absurdity. Let them be sure that every deed counts, that every word has power, and that we all can do our share to redeem the world in spite of all absurdities and all frustrations and all disappointments.

"And, above all, [let them] remember . . . to build a life as if it were a work of art."

Aged

Old age is something we are all anxious to attain. However, once attained we consider it a defeat, a form of capital punishment. In enabling us to reach old age, medical science may think that it gave us a blessing: however, we continue to act as if it were a disease.

More money and time are spent on the art of concealing the signs of old age than on the art of dealing with heart disease or cancer. You find more patients in the beauty parlors than in the hospitals. We would rather be bald than gray. A white hair is an abomination. Being old is a defeat, something to be ashamed of.

While we do not officially define old age as a second childhood, some of the programs we devise are highly effective in helping the aged to become children. . . . Now preoccupation with games and hobbies, the overemphasis on recreation, while certainly conducive to eliminating boredom temporarily, hardly contribute to inner strength. The effect is, rather, a pickled existence, preserved in brine with spices.

Is this the goal of existence: to study, grow, toil, mature, and to reach the age of retirement in order to live like a child? After all, *to be retired does not mean to be retarded.*

Old age is not a defeat but a victory, not a punishment but a privilege.

One ought to enter old age the way one enters the senior year at a university, in exciting anticipation of consummation. Rich in perspective, experienced in failure, the person advanced in years is capable of shedding prejudices and the fever of vested interests. He does not see anymore in every fellow man a person who stands in his way, and competitiveness may cease to be his way of thinking.

At every home for the aged there is a director of recreation in charge of physical activities; there ought to be also a director of learning in charge of intellectual activities. We insist upon minimum standards for physical well being, what about minimum standards for intellectual well being?

What the nation needs is senior universities, universities for the advanced in years where wise men should teach the potentially wise, where the purpose of learning is not a career, but where the purpose of learning is learning itself.

The goal is not to keep the old man busy, but to remind him that every moment is an opportunity for greatness. Inner purification is at least as important as hobbies and recreation.

Always

It takes three things to attain a sense of
significant being:
   God
   A Soul
   And a Moment.
And the three are always here.

To Be

Just to be is a blessing.
Just to live is holy.

To Obey

What Adam hears first is a command.

Against the conception of the world as something just here,
the Bible insists that the world is creation. Over all being
stand the words: Let there be! And there was, and there is.
To be is to obey the commandment of creation. God's word
is at stake in being. There is a cosmic piety in sheer being.
What is endures as a response to a command.

The Pious Man

Piety is the direct opposite of selfishness. Living as he does
in the vision of the unutterably pure, the pious man turns his
back on his own human vanity, and longs to surrender the

forces of egotism to the might of God. He is aware of both the shabbiness of human life and the meagerness and insufficiency of human service; and so, to protect the inner wholesomeness and purity of devotion from being defiled by interference from the petty self, he strives toward self-exclusion, self-forgetfulness and an inner anonymity of service. He desires to be unconscious that it is he who is consecrating himself to the service of God. The pious man lays no claim to reward. He hates show, or being conspicuous in any way, and is shy of displaying his qualities even to his own mind. He is engrossed in the beauty of that which he worships, and dedicates himself to ends the greatness of which exceeds his capacity for adoration.

The Pious Man

Piety is allegiance to the will of God. . . .

Life is a mandate, not the enjoyment of an annuity; a task, not a game; a command, not a favor. So to the pious man life never appears as a fatal chain of events following necessarily one on another, but comes as a voice with an appeal. It is a flow of opportunity for service, every experience giving the clue to a new duty, so that all that enters life is for him a means of showing renewed devotion. Piety is, thus, not an excess of enthusiasm, but implies a resolve to follow a definite course of life in pursuit of the will of God. All the pious man's thoughts and plans revolve around this concern, and nothing can distract him or turn him from the way.

Whoever sets out on this way soon learns how imperious is the spirit. He senses the compulsion to serve, and though at times he may attempt to escape, the strength of this compulsion will bring him back inevitably to the right way in search of the will of God. Before he acts, he will pause to weigh the effects of his act in the scales of God. Before he speaks, he will consider whether his words will be well pleasing to Him.

Thus, in self-conquest and earnest endeavor, with sacrifice and single-mindedness, through prayer and grace, he proceeds on his way, and to him the way is more important than the goal. It is not his destiny to accomplish but to contribute, and his will to serve shapes his entire conduct.

His preoccupation with the will of God is not limited to a section of his activities, but his great desire is to place his whole life at the disposal of God. In this he finds the real meaning of life. He would feel wretched and lost without the certainty that his life, insignificant though it be, is of some purpose in the great plan, and life takes on enhanced value when he feels himself engaged in fulfilling purposes which lead him away from himself.

In this way, he feels that in whatever he does, he is ascending step by step a ladder leading to the ultimate. In aiding a creature, he is helping the Creator. In succoring the poor, he fulfills a concern of God. In admiring the good, he reveres the spirit of God. In loving the pure, he is drawn to Him. In promoting the right, he is directing things toward His will, in which all aims must terminate. Ascending by this ladder, the pious man reaches the state of self-forgetfulness, sacrificing not only his desires but also his will; for he realizes that it is the will of God that matters, and not his own perfection or salvation. Thus, the glory of man's devotion to the good becomes a treasure of God on earth.

The Pious Man

Whatever the pious man does is linked to the divine; each smallest trifle is tangential to His course. In breathing he uses His force; in thinking he wields His power. He moves always under the unseen canopy of remembrance, and the wonderful weight of the name of God rests steadily on his mind. The word of God is as vital to him as air or food. He is never alone, never companionless, for God is within reach of his heart. . . . The pious man needs no miraculous communication to make him aware of God's presence; nor is a crisis necessary to awaken him to the meaning and appeal of that presence. His awareness may be overlaid momentarily or concealed by some violent shift in consciousness, but it never fades away. It is this awareness of ever living under the watchful eye of God that leads the pious man to see hints of God in the varied things he encounters in his daily walk; so that many a simple event can be accepted by him both for what it is and also as a gentle hint or kindly reminder of things divine. In this mindfulness he eats and drinks, works and plays, talks and thinks; for piety is a life compatible with God's presence.

Piety

Holiness does not signify an air that prevails in the solemn atmosphere of a sanctuary, a quality reserved for supreme acts, an adverb of the spiritual, the distinction of hermits and priests. . . . The strength of holiness lies underground, in the somatic. It is primarily in the way in which we gratify physical needs that the seed of holiness is planted. Originally the holy *(kadosh)* meant that which is set apart, isolated, segregated. In Jewish piety it assumed a new meaning, denoting a quality that is involved, immersed in common and earthly endeavors; carried primarily by individual, private, simple deeds rather than public ceremonies. . . .

A man alive, a flower blooming in the spring, is a fulfillment of God's command: "Let there be!" In living we are directly doing the will of God, in a way which is beyond choice or decision. This is why our very existence is contact with His will; why life is holy and a responsibility of God as well as man.

Poet or Pious

If a poet and a pious man
should confer and exchange views,
the poet would say:
"All he lives, I say";
and the pious man would know:
"All he says, I live."

Defiance of Despair

A religious man
is a person who holds God and man
in one thought at one time,
at all times,
who suffers in himself harms done to others,
whose greatest passion is compassion,
whose greatest strength is love
and defiance of despair.

No Religion Is an Island

. . . No religion is an island. We are all involved with one another. Spiritual betrayal on the part of one of us affects the faith of all of us. Views adopted in one community have an impact on other communities. Today religious isolationism is a myth. For all the profound differences in perspective and substance, Judaism is sooner or later affected by the intellectual, moral and spiritual events within the Christian society, and vice versa.

We fail to realize that while different exponents of faith in the world of religion continue to be wary of the ecumenical movement, there is another ecumenical movement, worldwide in extent and influence: nihilism. We must choose between interfaith and inter-nihilism. Cynicism is not parochial. Should religions insist upon the illusion of complete isolation? Should we refuse to be on speaking terms with one another and hope for each other's failure? Or whould we pray for each other's health, and help one another in preserving one's respective legacy, in preserving a common legacy?

Depth Theology

I suggest that the most significant basis for meeting of men of different religious traditions is the level of fear and trembling, of humility and contrition, where our individual moments of faith are mere waves in the endless ocean of mankind's reaching out for God, where all formulations and articulations appear as understatements, where our souls are swept away by the awareness of the urgency of answering

God's commandment, while stripped of pretension and conceit we sense the tragic insufficiency of human faith.

What divides us? . . .

We disagree in law and creed, in commitments which lie at the very heart of our religious existence. We say "No" to one another in some doctrines essential and sacred to us.

What unites us? Our being accountable to God, our being objects of God's concern, precious in His eyes.

Our conceptions of what ails us may be different; but the anxiety is the same. The language, the imagination, the concretization of our hopes are different, but the embarrassment is the same, and so is the sigh, the sorrow, and the necessity to obey.

We may disagree about the ways of achieving fear and trembling, but the fear and trembling are the same, and so is arrogance, iniquity. The proclamations are different, the callousness is the same. . . .

Above all, while dogmas and forms of worship are divergent, God is the same. . . .

There are moments when we all stand together and see our faces in the mirror: the anguish of humanity and its helplessness; the perplexity of the individual and the need of divine guidance; being called to praise and to do what is required.

Death

The greatest problem is not how to continue but how to exalt our existence. The cry for a life beyond the grave is presumptuous, if there is no cry for eternal life prior to our descending to the grave. Eternity is not perpetual future but perpetual presence. He has planted in us the seed of eternal life. The world to come is not only a hereafter but also a *herenow*.

Our greatest problem is not how to continue but how to return. "How can I repay unto the Lord all his bountiful dealings with me?" (Psalms 116:12). When life is an answer, death is a home-coming.

The deepest wisdom man can attain is to know that his destiny is to aid, to serve. We have to conquer in order to succumb; we have to acquire in order to give away; we have to triumph in order to be overwhelmed. Man has to understand in order to believe, to know in order to accept. . . .

This is the meaning of death: the ultimate self-dedication to the divine. Death so understood will not be distorted by the craving for immortality, for this act of giving away is reciprocity on man's part for God's gift of life.

For the pious man it is a privilege to die.

BIBLE

The Bible is holiness in words.

To Believe

To believe,
we need God,
a soul,
and the Word.

Being Beyond Mystery

It is through the prophets that we may be able to encounter Him as a Being who is beyond the mystery. In the prophets the ineffable became a voice, disclosing that God is not a being that is apart and away from ourselves, as ancient man believed, that He is not an enigma, but justice, mercy; not only a power to which we are accountable, but also a pattern for our lives. He is not the Unknown; He is the Father, the God of Abraham; out of the endless ages came compassion and guidance. Even the individual who feels forsaken remembers Him as the God of his fathers.

Mankind's Greatest Privilege

The Bible is mankind's greatest privilege.

It is so far off and so direct in its demands and full of compassion in its understanding. No other book so loves and respects the life of man. No loftier songs about his misery and hope have ever been expressed, and nowhere has man's need for guidance and the certainty of his ultimate redemption been so keenly conceived. It has the words that startle the guilty and the promise that upholds the forlorn. And he who seeks a language in which to utter his deepest concern, to pray, will find it in the Bible.

A Map of Time

There are no words in the world more knowing,
    more disclosing
        and more indispensable,
words both stern and graceful,
heart-rending and healing.
A truth so universal: God is One.
A thought so consoling: He is with us in distress.
A responsibility so overwhelming:
    his name can be desecrated.
A map of time: from creation to redemption.
Guideposts along the way: the Seventh Day.
An offering: contrition of the heart.
A utopia: would that all people were prophets.
The insight: man lives by his faithfulness;
his home is in time and his substance in deeds.
A standard so bold: ye shall be holy.

A commandment so daring: love thy neighbor as thyself.
A fact so sublime: human and divine pathos can be in
   accord.
And a gift so undeserved: the ability to repent.

The Story of Every Man

The Bible is not an end but a beginning; a precedent, not
a story. Its being embedded in particular historic situations
has not deterred it from being everlasting. Nothing in it is
surreptitious or trite. It is not an epic about the life of heroes
but the story of every man in all climates and all ages. Its
topic is the world, the whole of history, containing the pattern
of a constitution of a united mankind as well as guidance
toward establishing such a union. It shows the way to nations
as well as to individuals. It continues to scatter seeds of
justice and compassion, to echo God's cry to the world and
to pierce man's armor of callousness.

No Substitute

Why does the Bible surpass everything created by man?
Why is there no work worthy of comparison with it? Why is
there no substitute for the Bible, no parallel to the history it
has engendered? Why must all who seek the living God turn
to its pages?
Set the Bible beside any of the truly great books produced
by the genius of man, and see how they are diminished in
stature. The Bible shows no concern with literary form, with
verbal beauty, yet its absolute sublimity rings through all its

pages. Its lines are so monumental and at the same time so simple that whoever tries to compete with them produces either a commentary or a caricature. It is a work we do not know how to assess. The plummet line of scholarship cannot probe its depth nor will critical analysis ever grasp its essence. Other books you can estimate, you can measure, compare; the Bible you can only extol. Its insights surpass our standards. There is nothing greater.

Inexhaustible

Irrefutably, indestructibly, never wearied by time, the Bible wanders through the ages, giving itself with ease to all men, as if it belonged to every soul on earth. It speaks in every language and in every age. It benefits all the arts and does not compete with them. We all draw upon it, and it remains pure, inexhaustible and complete. In three thousand years it has not aged a day. It is a book that cannot die. Oblivion shuns its pages. Its power is not subsiding. In fact, it is still at the very beginning of its career, the full meaning of its content having hardly touched the threshold of our minds; like an ocean at the bottom of which countless pearls lie, waiting to be discovered, its spirit is still to be unfolded. Though its words seem plain and its idiom translucent, unnoticed meanings, undreamed-of intimations break forth constantly. More than two thousand years of reading and research have not succeeded in exploring its full meaning. Today it is as if it had never been touched, never been seen, as if we had not even begun to read it.

The Prophet

The prophet is a man who feels fiercely. God has thrust a burden upon his soul, and he is bowed and stunned at man's fierce greed. Frightful is the agony of man; no human voice can convey its full terror. Prophecy is the voice that God has lent to the silent agony, a voice to the plundered poor, to the profaned riches of the world. It is a form of living, a crossing point of God and man.

God is raging in the prophet's words.

Only Witnesses

There are no proofs for the existence of the God of Abraham. There are only witnesses. The greatness of the prophet lies not only in the ideas he expressed, but also in the moments he experienced. The prophet is a witness, and his words a testimony.

Prophecy

God is invisible, distant, dwelling in darkness (I Kings 8:12). His thoughts are not our thoughts; His ways in history are shrouded and perplexing. Prophecy is a moment of unshrouding, an opening of the eyes, a lifting of the curtain. Such moments are rare in history. . . . It was as if God had opened a door: in the prophets His word was revealed. . . . Not forever, the prophet is told. The Lord will shut the door, and the word will obtrude no more. . . .

And yet, the word of God never comes to an end. For this reason, prophetic predictions are seldom final. No word is God's final word. Judgment, far from being absolute, is conditional. A change in man's conduct brings about a change in God's judgment. No word is God's final word.

Sacred Deeds

Pagans exalt sacred things.
The prophets extoll sacred deeds.

Trivialities

In biblical days prophets were astir while the world was asleep; today the world is astir while church and synagogue are busy with trivialities.

God's Anthropology

The Bible is primarily not man's vision of God
but God's vision of man.
The Bible is not man's theology
but God's anthropology.

God in Search of Man

All of human history as seen by the Bible is the history of *God in search of man*. In spite of man's failure, over and over, God does not abandon His hope to find righteous men. Adam,

Cain, the generation of the flood, the generation of the Tower of Babel—it is a story of failure and defiance. And yet, God did not abandon man, hoping against hope to see a righteous world. Noah was saved in the expectation that out of his household generations would not corrupt their ways, and a covenant was established with him and his descendants after him. But it was Noah himself who planted a vineyard and then became drunk. It was Noah himself who set brother against brother, blessing Shem and Yapheth, and cursing Canaan to be a slave to his brothers. The arrogance of those who built the Tower of Babel paved the way for greater tension and confusion. But the Lord did not abandon man, and in His search determined to choose Abraham, so that in him might "all the families of the earth be blessed."

Impatience with Injustice

Turning from the discourses of the great metaphysicians to the orations of the prophets, one may feel as if he were going down from the realm of the sublime to an area of trivialities. Instead of dealing with the timeless issues of being and becoming, of matter and form, of definitions and demonstrations, one is thrown into orations about widows and orphans, about the corruption of judges and affairs of the market place. The prophets make so much ado about paltry things, employing the most excessive language in speaking about flimsy subjects. So what if somewhere in ancient Palestine poor people have not been treated properly by the rich? . . . Why such immoderate excitement? Why such intense indignation?

Their breathless impatience with injustice may strike us as

hysteria. We ourselves witness continually acts of injustice, manifestations of hypocrisy, falsehood, outrage, misery, but we rarely get indignant or overly excited. To the prophets a minor, commonplace sort of injustice assumes almost cosmic proportions.

Human and Holy

He who seeks an answer to the most pressing question, what is living? will find an answer in the Bible: man's destiny is to be a partner rather than a master.

There is a task, a law, and a way: the task is redemption, the law, to do justice, to love mercy, and the way is the secret of being *human and holy*.

When we are gasping with despair, when the wisdom of science and the splendor of the arts fail to save us from fear and the sense of futility, the Bible offers us the only hope:

History is a circuitous way for the steps of the Messiah.

On Sinai

What happened on Sinai?

The Bible tries to say it in two ways. What it says in one is something words can hardly bear: "The Lord came down upon Mount Sinai" (Exodus 19:20). No sentence in the world has ever said more: He who is beyond, hidden and exalted above space and time was humbly here, for all Israel to sense.

But the Bible also speaks in another way: "I have talked to you from heaven" (Exodus 20:22). He did not descend upon the earth; all that happened was that His word welled "from heaven."

These passages do not contradict each other; they refer not to one but to two events. For *revelation was both an event to God and an event to man*. Indeed, in the second passage it is God who speaks (in the first person); the first passage conveys what the people experienced (it speaks of God in the third person). The same act had two aspects. God did and did not descend upon the earth. The voice came out of heaven but man heard it out of Sinai.

The Good and the Holy

There is much that philosophy could learn from the Bible. To the philosopher the idea of the good is the most exalted idea. But to the Bible the idea of the good is penultimate; it cannot exist without the holy. The holy is the essence, the good is its expression. Things created in six days He considered *good*, the seventh day He made *holy*.

About Us

We have so much to say about the Bible that we are not prepared to hear what the Bible has to say about us.

The Bible Is an Answer

The Bible is an answer to the supreme question: *what does God demand of us?* Yet the question has gone out of the world. God is portrayed as a mass of vagueness behind a veil

81

of enigmas, and His voice has become alien to our minds, to our hearts, to our souls. We have learned to listen to every "I" except the "I" of God. The man of our time may proudly declare: nothing animal is alien to me but everything divine is. This is the status of the Bible in modern life: it is a sublime answer, but we do not know the question any more. Unless we recover the question, there is no hope of understanding the Bible.

Answer or Refuse

Vain would be any attempt to reconstruct the hidden circumstances under which a word of God alarmed a prophet's soul. Who could uncover the divine data or piece together the strange perceptions of a Moses? The prophet did not leave information behind. All we have is the prophet's certainty, endless awe and appreciation. All we have is a Book, and all we can do is to try to sense the unworded across its words.

What actually transpired is as unimaginable to us as it was unbelievable to those who witnessed it. We cannot comprehend it. We can only answer it. Or refuse to answer.

God in Search of Man, pp. 188–89

Flowers but No Fruits

Socrates taught us that a life without thinking is not worth living. Now, thinking is a noble effort, but the finest thinking may end in futility. In thinking, man is left to himself;

he may soar into astral space and proclaim the finest thoughts; yet what will be the echo and what its meaning for the soul?

The Bible taught us that life without commitment is not worth living; that thinking without roots will bear flowers but no fruits. Our commitment is to God, and our roots are in the prophetic events of Israel.

More Than an Idea

> Let justice roll down like waters,
> And righteousness like a mighty stream.
> (Amos 5:24)

Righteousness as a mere tributary, feeding human interests, is easily exhausted and more easily abused. But righteousness is not a trickle; it is God's power in the world, a torrent, an impetuous drive, full of grandeur and majesty. The surge is choked, the sweep is blocked. Yet the mighty stream will break all dikes.

Justice, people seem to agree, is a principle, a norm, an ideal of the highest importance. We all insist that it ought to be—but it may not be. In the eyes of the prophets, justice is more than an idea or a norm: justice is charged with the omnipotence of God. What ought to be, shall be!

Prophecy

Patient, pliant, and submissive to our minds is the world of nature, but obstinately silent. We adore her wealth and tacit wisdom, we tediously decipher her signs, but she never speaks to us. Or do we expect the stars to understand us or the sea to be persuaded? Communication is an act contingent upon so many intricate and complex conditions that the idea of nature addressing herself to man is inconceivable. Communication would not only presuppose her being endowed with a soul, but also man's possessing a mental capacity to understand her specific signs of communication.

Still, the prophetic claim that the eternal God addressed Himself to a mortal mind is not inimical to reason. The very structure of matter is made possible by the way in which the endless crystallizes in the smallest. If the stream of energy that is stored up in the sun and the soil can be channeled into a blade of grass, why should it be a priori excluded that the spirit of God reached into the minds of men?

There is such a distance between the sun and a flower. Can a flower, worlds away from the source of energy, attain a perception of its origin? Can a drop of water ever soar to behold, even for a moment, the stream's distant source? In prophecy it is as if the sun communed with the flower, as if the source sent out a current to reach a drop.

The Word of God

Revelation means that the thick silence which fills the endless distance between God and the human mind was pierced, and man was told that God is concerned with the affairs of man; that not only does man need God, God is also in need of man.

It is such knowledge that makes the soul of Israel immune to despair.

Here truth is not timeless and detached from the world but a way of living and involved in all acts of God and man.

The word of God is not an object of contemplation. The word of God must become history.

Thus the word of God entered the world of man; not an "ought to," an idea suspended between being and non-being, a shadow of the will, a concession of the mind, but a perpetual event, a demand of God more real than a mountain, more powerful than all thunders.

The Quest for the Righteous Man

The spirit of philosophy has often been characterized as the quest of values, as a search for that which is of greatest value. What is the spirit of the Bible? Its concern is not with the abstract concept of disembodied values, detached from concrete existence. Its concern is with man and his relation to the will of God. The Bible is the quest for the righteous man, for a righteous people.

> The Lord looks down from heaven upon the children of man, to see if there are any that act wisely, that seek after God. They have all gone astray, they are all alike corrupt; there is none that does good, no, not one. (Psalms 14:2–3)

The incidents recorded in the Bible to the discerning eye are episodes of one great drama: the quest of God for man; His search for man, and man's flight from Him.

Last Word

The word of God
never comes to an end.
No word
is
God's last word.

HOLY DEEDS

The Mitzvah

It is not said: Ye shall be full of awe for I am holy, but: "Ye shall be holy, for I the Lord your God am holy" (Leviticus 19:2).

How does a human being, "dust and ashes," turn holy? Through doing His mitsvot, His commandments.

"The Holy God is sanctified through righteousness" (Isaiah 5:16).

A man to be holy must fear his mother and father, keep the Sabbath, not turn to idols . . . nor deal falsely nor lie to one another . . . not curse the deaf nor put a stumbling-block before the blind . . . not be guilty of any injustice . . . not be a tale-bearer . . . not stand idly by the blood of your neighbor . . . not hate . . . not take vengeance nor bear any grudge . . . but love thy neighbor as thyself (Leviticus 19:3–18).

We live by the conviction that acts of goodness reflect the hidden light of His holiness. His light is above our minds but not beyond our will. It is within our power to mirror His unending love in deeds of kindness, like brooks that hold the sky.

The Cult

A mitzvah is performed when a deed is outdone by a sigh, when Divine reference is given to a human fact. In a mitzvah we give the source of an act, rather than the underlining of a word. Ceremonies are performed for the sake of onlookers; mitzvot are done for the sake of God. Ceremonies must be visible, spectacular; a mitzvah is spurious when turning impressive.

Mitzvot are sanctifications rather than ceremonies. Without faith, the festivities turn dull and artificial. The esthetic satisfaction they offer is meager compared, e.g., with that of listening to a symphony. . . .

Moses was not concerned with initiating a new cult, but with creating a new people. In the center of Jewish living is not a cult but observance [of mitzvot]; the former is a realm of its own, the latter comprises all of life. Since the destruction of the Temple in Jerusalem, Judaism has had a minimum of cult and a maximum of observance. The prophetic fight against the mendacity of spurious ceremonies has left its trace in our lives. There is a minimum of show, of ceremonialism in Jewish religion, even in public worship. Ceremonies are for the eye, but Judaism is an appeal to the spirit. The only ceremony still observed in the synagogue is the blessing of the priests—but then the congregation is required to close its eyes.

Our Task

God is hiding in the world.
Our task is to let the divine emerge from our deeds.

Proximity to the Sacred

Life passes on in proximity to the sacred, and it is this proximity that endows existence with ultimate significance. In our relation to the immediate we touch upon the most distant. Even the satisfaction of physical needs can be a sacred act. Perhaps the essential message of Judaism is that in doing the finite we may perceive the infinite.

Theology of the Common Deed

"The gods attend to great matters; they neglect small ones," Cicero maintains. According to Aristotle, the gods are not concerned at all with the dispensation of good and bad fortune or external things. To the Hebrew prophet, however, no subject is as worthy of consideration as the plight of man. Indeed, God Himself is described as reflecting over the plight of man rather than as contemplating eternal ideas. His mind is preoccupied with man, with the concrete actualities of history rather than with the timeless issues of thought. In the prophet's message, nothing that has bearing upon good and evil is small or trite in the eyes of God.

The teaching of Judaism is the *theology of the common deed*. The Bible insists that God is *concerned with everydayness, with the trivialities of life*. The great challenge does not lie in organizing solemn demonstrations, but in how we manage the commonplace. The prophet's field of concern is not the mysteries of heaven, the glories of eternity, but the blights of society, the affairs of the market place. He addresses himself to those who trample upon the needy, who increase the price of grain, use dishonest scales, and sell the refuse of corn

(Amos 8:4–6). The predominant feature of the biblical pattern of life is unassuming, unheroic, inconspicuous piety, the sanctification of trifles, attentiveness to details.

"The wages of a hired servant shall not abide with thee all night until the morning" (Leviticus 19:13). Don't delay the payment due to him. "If you meet your enemy's ox or his ass going astray, you shall bring it back to him. If you see the ass of one who hates you lying under its burden . . . help him to lift it up" (Exodus 23:4–5). "When you build a new house, you shall make a parapet for your roof," to prevent anyone from falling from it (Deuteronomy 22:8).

Routine

Being bound to an order and stability of observance, to a discipline of worship at set hours and fixed forms is a celestial routine. Nature does not cease to be natural because of its being subject to regularity of seasons. Loyalty to external forms, dedication of the will is itself a form of worship. The mitsvot sustain their halo even when our minds forget to light in us the attentiveness to the holy. The path of loyalty to the routine of sacred living runs along the borderline of the spirit; though being outside, one remains very close to the spirit. Routine holds us in readiness for the moments in which the soul enters into accord with the spirit.

While love is hibernating, our loyal deeds speak. It is right that the good actions should become a habit, that the preference of justice should become our second nature.

A good person is not he who does the right thing, but he who is in the habit of doing the right thing.

To Meet the Spirit

Inspirations are brief, sporadic and rare. In the long interims the mind is often dull, bare and vapid. There is hardly a soul that can radiate more light than it receives. To perform a mitzvah is to meet the spirit. But the spirit is not something we can acquire once and for all but something we must constantly live with and pray for. For this reason the Jewish way of life is to reiterate the ritual, to meet the spirit again and again, the spirit in oneself and the spirit that hovers over all beings.

The spirit rests not only on our achievement, on our goal, but also on our effort, on our way. This is why the very act of going to the house of worship, every day or every seventh day, is a song without words. When done in humility, in simplicity of heart, it is like a child who, eager to hear a song, spreads out the score before its mother.

A Leap of Action

A Jew is asked to take a leap of action rather than a leap of thought. He is asked to surpass his needs, to do more than he understands in order to understand more than he does. In carrying out the word of the Torah he is ushered into the presence of spiritual meaning. Through the ecstasy of deeds he learns to be certain of the hereness of God. Right living is a way to right thinking.

To Accept the Law

Man had to be expelled from the Garden of Eden;
he had to witness the murder of half of the
    human species by Cain;
        experience the catastrophe of the Flood;
            the confusion of the languages;
                slavery in Egypt
                    and the wonder of the Exodus,
to be ready to accept the law.

Polarity

Jewish thinking and living can only be adequately under-stood in terms of a dialectic pattern, containing opposite or contrasted properties. As in a magnet, the ends of which have opposite magnetic qualities, these terms are opposite to one another and exemplify a polarity which lies at the very heart of Judaism, the polarity of ideas and events, of mitsvah and sin, of kavanah and deed, of regularity and spontaneity, of uniformity and individuality, of halacha and agada, of law and inwardness, of love and fear, of understanding and obedience, of joy and discipline, of the good and the evil drive, of time and eternity, of this world and the world to come, of revelation and response, of insight and information, of empathy and self-expression, of creed and faith, of the word and that which is beyond words, of man's quest for God and God in search of man. Even God's relation to the world is characterized by the polarity of justice and mercy, providence and concealment, the promise of reward and the demand to serve Him for His sake.

Taken abstractedly, all these terms seem to be mutually exclusive, yet in actual living they involve each other; the separation of the two is fatal to both. There is no halacha without agada, and no agada without halacha. We must neither disparage the body, nor sacrifice the spirit. The body is the discipline, the pattern, the law; the spirit is inner devotion, spontaneity, freedom. The body without the spirit is a corpse; the spirit without the body is a ghost. Thus a mitsvah is both a discipline and an inspiration, an act of obedience and an experience of joy, a yoke and a prerogative.

Our task is to learn how to maintain a harmony between the demands of halacha and the spirit of agada.

THE PEOPLE

Plucked from the Fire

I speak as a member of a congregation whose founder was Abraham, and the name of my rabbi is Moses.

I speak as a person who was able to leave Warsaw, the city in which I was born, just six weeks before the disaster began. My destination was New York, it would have been Auschwitz or Treblinka. I am a brand plucked from the fire, in which my people was burned to death. . . .

I speak as a person who is often afraid lest God has turned away from [man] in disgust.

Tragic or Holy

There is a high cost of living to be paid by a Jew. He has to be exalted in order to be normal in a world that is neither propitious for nor sympathetic to his survival. Some of us, tired of sacrifice and exertion, often wonder: Is Jewish existence worth the price? Others are overcome with panic; they are perplexed, and despair of recovery.

In trying to understand Jewish existence a Jewish philosopher must look for agreement with the men of Sinai as well as with the people of Auschwitz.

We are the most challenged people under the sun. Our existence is either superfluous or indispensable to the world; it is either tragic or holy to be a Jew.

The Mark of Cain

Emblazoned over the gates of the world in which we live is the escutcheon of the demons. The mark of Cain in the face of man has come to overshadow the likeness of God. There has never been so much guilt and distress, agony, and terror. At no time has the earth been so soaked with blood. Fellowmen turned out to be evil ghosts, monstrous and weird. Ashamed and dismayed, we ask: Who is responsible?

History is a pyramid of efforts and errors; yet at times it is the Holy Mountain on which God holds judgment over the nations. Few are privileged to discern God's judgment in history. But all may be guided by the words of the Baal Shem: If a man has beheld evil, he may know that it was shown to him in order that he learn his own guilt and repent; for what is shown to him is also within him.

We have trifled with the name of God. We have taken the ideals in vain. We have called for the Lord. He came. And was ignored. We have preached but eluded Him. We have praised but defied Him. Now we reap the fruits of our failure. Through centuries His voice cried in the wilderness. How skillfully it was trapped and imprisoned in the temples! How often it was drowned or distorted! Now we behold how it gradually withdraws, abandoning one people after another, departing from their souls, despising their wisdom. The taste for the good has all but gone from the earth. Men heap spite upon cruelty, malice upon atrocity.

The horrors of our time fill our souls with reproach and everlasting shame. We have profaned the word of God, and we have given the wealth of our land, the ingenuity of our minds and the dear lives of our youth to tragedy and perdition. There has never been more reason for man to be ashamed than now. Silence hovers mercilessly over many dreadful lands. The day of the Lord is a day without the Lord. Where is God? Why didst Thou not halt the trains loaded with Jews being led to slaughter? It is so hard to rear a child, to nourish and to educate. Why dost Thou make it so easy to kill? Like Moses, we hide our face; for we are afraid to look upon *Elohim*, upon His power of judgment. Indeed, where were we when men learned to hate in the days of starvation? When raving madmen were sowing wrath in the hearts of the unemployed?

Let modern dictatorship not serve as an alibi for our conscience. We have failed to fight *for* right, *for* justice, *for* goodness; as a result we must fight *against* wrong, *against* injustice, *against* evil. We have failed to offer sacrifices on the altar of peace; thus we offered sacrifices on the altar of war. A tale is told of a band of inexperienced mountain climbers. Without guides, they struck recklessly into the wilderness. Suddenly a rocky ledge gave way beneath their feet and they tumbled headlong into a dismal pit. In the darkness of the pit they recovered from their shock only to find themselves set upon by a swarm of angry snakes. For each snake the desperate men slew, ten more seemed to lash out in its place. Strangely enough, one man seemed to stand aside from the fight. When indignant voices of his struggling companions reproached him for not fighting, he called back: "If we remain here, we shall be dead before the snakes. I am searching for a way of escape from the pit for all of us."

Our world seems not unlike a pit of snakes. We did not

sink into the pit in 1939, or even in 1933. We had descended into it generations ago, and the snakes have sent their venom into the bloodstream of humanity, gradually paralyzing us, numbing nerve after nerve, dulling our minds, darkening our vision. Good and evil, that were once as real as day and night, have become a blurred mist. In our everyday life we worshiped force, despised compassion, and obeyed no law but our unappeasable appetite. The vision of the sacred has all but died in the soul of man. And when greed, envy and the reckless will to power came to maturity, the serpents cherished in the bosom of our civilization broke out of their dens to fall upon the helpless nations.

The outbreak of war was no surprise. It came as a long expected sequel to a spiritual disaster. Instilled with the gospel that truth is mere advantage and reverence weakness, people succumbed to the bigger advantage of a lie—"the Jew is our misfortune"—and to the power of arrogance—"tomorrow the whole world shall be ours," "the peoples' democracies must depend upon force." The roar of bombers over Rotterdam, Warsaw, London, was but the echo of thoughts bred for years by individual brains, and later applauded by entire nations. It was through our failure that people started to suspect that science is a device for exploitation; parliaments pulpits for hypocrisy, and religion a pretext for a bad conscience. In the tantalized souls of those who had faith in ideals, suspicion became a dogma and contempt the only solace. Mistaking the abortions of their conscience for intellectual heroism, many thinkers employ clever pens to scold and to scorn the reverence for life, the awe for truth, the loyalty to justice. Man, about to hang himself, discovers it is easier to hang others.

The conscience of the world was destroyed by those who were wont to blame others rather than themselves. Let us remember. We revered the instincts but distrusted the prophets. We labored to perfect engines and let our inner life go to wreck. We ridiculed superstition until we lost our ability to believe. We have helped to extinguish the light our fathers had kindled. We have bartered holiness for convenience, loyalty for success, love for power, wisdom for information, tradition for fashion.

We cannot dwell at ease under the sun of our civilization as our ancestors thought we could. What was in the minds of our martyred brothers in their last hours? They died with disdain and scorn for a civilization in which the killing of civilians could become a carnival of fun, for a civilization which gave us mastery over the forces of nature but lost control over the forces of our self.

Tanks and planes cannot redeem humanity, nor the discovery of guilt by association nor suspicion. A man with a gun is like a beast without a gun. The killing of snakes will save us for the moment but not forever. The war has outlasted the victory of arms as we failed to conquer the infamy of the soul: the indifference to crime, when committed against others. For evil is indivisible. It is the same in thought and in speech, in private and in social life. The greatest task of our time is to take the souls of men out of the pit. The world has experienced that God is involved. Let us forever remember that the sense for the sacred is as vital to us as the light of the sun. There can be no nature without spirit, no world without the Torah, no brotherhood without a father, no humanity without attachment to God.

God will return to us when we shall be willing to let Him in—into our banks and factories, into our Congress and clubs, into our courts and investigating committees, into our homes and theaters. For God is everywhere or nowhere, the Father of all men or no man, concerned about everything or nothing. Only in His presence shall we learn that the glory of man is not in his will to power, but in his power of compassion. Man reflects either the image of His presence or that of a beast.

Soldiers in the horror of battle offer solemn testimony that life is not a hunt for pleasure, but an engagement for service; that there are things more valuable than life; that the world is not a vacuum. Either we make it an altar for God or it is invaded by demons. There can be no neutrality. Either we are ministers of the sacred or slaves of evil. Let the blasphemy of our time not become an eternal scandal. Let future generations not loathe us for having failed to preserve what prophets and saints, martyrs and scholars have created in thousands of years. The apostles of force have shown that they are great in evil. Let us reveal that we can be as great in goodness. We will survive if we shall be as fine and sacrificial in our homes and offices, in our Congress and clubs, as our soldiers are on the fields of battle.

There is a divine dream which the prophets and rabbis have cherished and which fills our prayers, and permeates the acts of true piety. It is the dream of a world, rid of evil by the grace of God as well as by the efforts of man, by his dedication to the task of establishing the kingship of God in the world. God is waiting for us to redeem the world. We should not spend our life hunting for trivial satisfactions while God is waiting constantly and keenly for our effort and devotion.

The Almighty has not created the universe that we may have opportunities to satisfy our greed, envy and ambition. We have not survived that we may waste our years in vulgar vanities. The martyrdom of millions demands that we consecrate ourselves to the fulfillment of God's dream of salvation. Israel did not accept the Torah of their own free will. When

Israel approached Sinai, God lifted up the mountain and held it over their heads, saying: "Either you accept the Torah or be crushed beneath the mountain."

The mountain of history is over our heads again. Shall we renew the covenant with God?

Too Late

. . . A child of seven was reading in school the chapter which tells of the sacrifice of Isaac:

Isaac was on the way to Mount Moriah with his father; then he lay on the altar, bound, waiting to be sacrificed. My heart began to beat even faster; it actually sobbed with pity for Isaac. Behold, Abraham now lifted the knife. And now my heart froze within me with fright. Suddenly, the voice of the angel was heard: "Abraham, lay not your hand upon the lad, for now I know that you fear God." And here I broke out in tears and wept aloud. "Why are you crying?" asked the rabbi. "You know that Isaac was not killed."

And I said to him, still weeping, "But, rabbi, supposing the angel had come a second too late?"

The rabbi comforted me and calmed me by telling me that an angel cannot come late.

An angel cannot be late, but man, made of flesh and blood, may be.

History's Secret

The people of Israel groaned in distress. Out of Egypt, the land of plentiful food, they were driven into the wilderness. Their souls were dried away; there was nothing at all: no flesh to eat, no water to drink. All they had was a promise: to be led to the land of milk and honey. They were almost ready to stone Moses. "Wherefore hast thou brought us up out of Egypt, to kill us and our children and our cattle with thirst?" they cried. But, after they had worshipped the golden calf—when God had decided to detach Himself from His people, not to dwell any more in their midst, but to entrust an angel with the task of leading them out of the wilderness to the Promised Land—Moses exclaimed: "If Thou Thyself dost not go with us, take us not out of the wilderness" (Exodus 33:15).

This, perhaps, is the secret of our history: *to choose to remain in the wilderness rather than to be abandoned by Him.*

Israel

Judaism is not only the adherence to particular doctrines and observances, but primarily living in the spiritual order of the Jewish people, the living *in* the Jews of the past and *with* the Jews of the present. . . . It is not a doctrine, an idea, a faith, but the covenant between God and the people. Our share in holiness we acquire by living in the Jewish community. What we do as individuals is a trivial episode; what we attain as Israel causes us to become a part of eternity.

Israel and Mankind

Israel is the tree, we are the leaves. It is the clinging to the stem that keeps us alive. There has perhaps never been more need of Judaism than in our time, a time in which many cherished hopes of humanity lie crushed. We should be pioneers as were our fathers three thousand years ago. The future of all men depends upon their realizing that the sense of holiness is as vital as health. By following the Jewish way of life we maintain that sense and preserve the light for mankind's future visions.

The Track of God

Judaism is the track of God in the wilderness of oblivion. By being what we are, namely Jews; by attuning our own yearning to the lonely holiness in this world, we will aid humanity more than by any particular service we may render.

Belonging to Israel

Belonging to Israel is in itself a spiritual act. It is utterly inconvenient to be a Jew. The very survival of our people is a *kiddush hashem*. We live in spite of peril. Our very existence is a refusal to surrender to normalcy, to security and comfort. Experts in assimilation, the Jews could have diseappeared even before the names of modern nations were known.

To Ennoble the Common

Judaism is a theology of the common deed, . . . dealing not so much with the training for the exceptional, as with the management of the trivial. The predominant feature in the Jewish pattern of life is unassuming, inconspicuous piety rather than extravagance, mortification, asceticism. Thus, the purpose seems to be to ennoble the common, to endow worldly things with hieratic beauty; to attune the comparative to the absolute, to associate the detail with the whole, to adapt our own being with its plurality, conflicts and contradictions, to the all-transcending unity, to the holy.

A Memory of Moments

The essence of Jewish religious thinking does not lie in entertaining a concept of God but in the ability to articulate a memory of moments of illumination by His presence. Israel is not a people of definers but a people of witnesses: "Ye are My witnesses" (Isaiah 43:10). Reminders of what has been disclosed to us are hanging over our souls like stars, remote and of mind-surpassing grandeur. They shine through dark and dangerous ages, and their reflection can be seen in the lives of those who guard the path of conscience and memory in the wilderness of careless living.

Since those perennial reminders have moved into our minds, wonder has never left us. Heedfully we stare through the telescope of ancient rites lest we lose the perpetual brightness beckoning to our souls. Our mind has not kindled the flame, has not produced these principles. Still our thoughts glow with their light.

Named for God

We have never been the same since the day on which the voice of God overwhelmed us at Sinai. It is for ever impossible for us to retreat into an age that predates the Sinaitic event. Something unprecedented happened. God revealed His name to us, and we are named after Him. "All the peoples of the earth shall see that you are called by the name of the Lord" (Deuteronomy 28:10).

There are two Hebrew names for Jew: *Yehudi*, the first three letters of which are the first three letters of the Ineffable Name, and Israel, the end of which, *el*, means God in Hebrew.

Two Poles

We live between two historic poles:
Sinai and the Kingdom of God.

Summoned

We do not live in a void. We never suffer from a fear of roaming about in the emptiness of Time. We own the past and are, hence, not afraid of what is to be. We remember where we came from. We were summoned and cannot forget it, winding the clock of eternal history.

Jewish Philosophy

The task of Jewish philosophy is to make our thinking compatible with our destiny.

A Holy People

What we have learned from Jewish history is that if a man is not more than human then he is less than human. Judaism is an attempt to prove that in order to be a man, you have to be more than a man, that in order to be a people we have to be more than a people. Israel was made to be a "holy people."

The Covenant of Abraham

The term "God of Abraham, Isaac, and Jacob" is semantically different from a term such as "the God of truth, goodness and beauty." Abraham, Isaac, and Jacob do not signify ideas, principles or abstract values. Nor do they stand for teachers or thinkers, and the term is not to be understood like that of "the God of Kant, Hegel, and Schelling."

Abraham, Isaac, and Jacob are not principles to be comprehended but lives to be continued. The life of him who joins the covenant of Abraham continues the life of Abraham. For the present is not apart from the past. "Abraham is still standing before God" (Genesis 18:22). Abraham endures forever.

We *are* Abraham, Isaac, Jacob.

Space and Time

Most of us succumb to the magnetic property of things and evaluate events by their tangible results. We appreciate things that are displayed in the realm of Space. The truth,

104

however, is that the genuinely precious is encountered in the realm of Time, rather than in Space. Monuments of bronze live by the grace of the memory of those who gaze at their form, while moments of the soul endure even when banished to the back of the mind. Feelings, thoughts, are our own, while possessions are alien and often treacherous to the self. To be is more essential than to have. Though we deal with things, we live in deeds.

Pagans exalt sacred things, the Prophets extol sacred deeds. The most precious object that has ever been on earth were the Two Tablets of stone which Moses received upon Mount Sinai: "The tablets were the work of God, and the writing was the writing of God, graven upon the tablets," But when coming down the mount—the Two Tablets he had just received in his hands—Moses saw the people dance around the Golden Calf, he cast the Tablets out of his hands and broke them before their eyes.

The stone is broken, but the Words are alive. The replica Moses had subsequently made is gone too, but the Words did not die. They still knock at our gates as if begging to be engraved "on the Tablets of every heart." While others have carried their piety, fervor, faith into magnificent songs of architecture, our ancestors had neither the skill nor the material necessary to produce comparable structures. Phoenician craftsman had to be brought to Jerusalem by Solomon the King to assist in erecting the Temple for the Lord. But there were Jews who knew how to lay bricks in the soul, to rear holiness made of simple deeds, of study and prayer, of care, of fear and love. They knew how to pattern and raise a pyramid that no one could see but God.

Constant Vigilance

We must understand the sense of values that characterized the East European Jews in order to appraise the fact that their best intellects were devoted to the study, interpretation, and development of the Torah. In their eyes, the world was not a derelict which the creator had abandoned to chance. Life to them was not an opportunity for indulgence, but a mission entrusted to every individual, an enterprise at least as responsible, for example, as the management of a factory. Every man constantly produces thoughts, words, deeds, committing them either to the powers of holiness or the powers of impurity. He is constantly engaged either in building or in destroying. But his task is to restore, by fulfilling the Torah, what has been impaired in the cosmos, to labor in the service of the cosmos for the sake of God.

The East European scholar was rarely dominated by a desire for austere rigorism or a liking for irrational discipline as a purpose in itself. In the main, he was inspired by a sense of the importance of his mission and by the conviction that the world could not exist without the Torah. This sense lent his life the quality of an artistic act, the medium of which is not stone or bronze, but the mystic substance of the universe.

Scientists dedicate their lives to the study of the habits of insects or the properties of plants. To them every trifle is significant; they inquire diligently into the most intricate qualities of things. But the pious Ashkenazic scholars investigated just as passionately the laws that ought to govern human conduct. . . . Wishing to banish the chaos of human existence and to civilize the life of man according to the Torah, they trembled over every move, every breath; no detail was treated lightly—everything was serious. Just as the self-sacrificing devotion of the scientist seems torture to the debauchee, so the poetry of rigorism jars on the ears of the cynic. But, perhaps, the question of what benediction to pronounce upon a certain type of food, the problem of matching the material with the spiritual, is more important than is generally imagined.

Man has not advanced very far from the coast of chaos. A frantic call to disorder shrieks in the world. Where is the power that can offset the effect of that alluring call? The world cannot remain a vacuum. We are all either ministers of the sacred or slaves of evil. The only safeguard against constant danger is constant vigilance, constant guidance.

A Prince

It was not by accident that the Jews of Eastern Europe thought little of worldy education. They resisted the stream of enlightenment which threatened to engulf the small province of Jewishness. They did not despise science. They believed, however, that a bit of spiritual nobility was a thousand times more valuable than all the secular sciences, that praying three times a day "My God, guard my tongue from evil" was more important than the study of physics, that meditating upon the Psalms filled man with more compassion than the study of Roman history.

They put no trust in the secular world. They believed that the existence of the world was not contingent on museums and libraries, but on houses of worship and study. To them, the house of study was not important because the world needed it, but, on the contrary, the world was important because houses of study existed in it. To them, life without the Torah and without piety was chaos, and a man who lived without these was looked upon with a sense of fear. They realized quite well that the world was full of ordeals and dangers, that it contained Cain's jealousy of Abel, the cold malevolence of Sodom, and the hatred of Esau, but they also knew that there was in it the charity of Abraham and the tenderness of Rachel.

Harassed and oppressed, they carried deep within their hearts a contempt for the "world," with its power and pomp, with its bustling and boasting. People who at midnight lamented the glory of God that is in exile and spent their days peddling onions were not insulted by the scorn of their enemies nor impressed by their praises. They knew that the Jews were in exile, that the world was unredeemed. . . . Outwardly a Jew might have been a pauper, but inwardly he felt like a prince, a kin to the king of kings. Unconquerable freedom was in him who, when wrapped in *tallith* and *tefillin*, consecrated his soul to the sanctification of the Holy Name.

The Little Candles

In the spiritual confusion of the last hundred years, many of us overlooked the incomparable beauty of our old, poor homes. Dazzled by the lights of the metropolis, the luminous visions that for so many generations shone in the little candles were extinguished for some of us.

In our zeal to change we ridiculed superstition until we lost our ability to believe. We have helped to extinguish the light our fathers had kindled. We have bartered holiness for convenience, loyalty for success, wisdom for information, prayers for sermons, tradition for fashion.

Judaism today is the least known religion. Its rare splendor has been so frequently adjusted to the trivialities of changing opinions that what is left is a commonplace. There are only few who still perceive the vanishing *niggun* of its perennial yearning.

A Vanished World

A world has vanished. All that remains is a sanctuary hidden in the realm of spirit. We of this generation are still holding the key. Unless we remember, unless we unlock it, the holiness of ages will remain a secret of God. We of this generation are still holding the key—the key to the sanctuary which is also the shelter of our own deserted souls. If we mislay the key, we shall elude ourselves.

In this hour we, the living, are "the people of Israel." The tasks, begun by the patriarchs and prophets and continued by their descendants, are now entrusted to us. We are either the last Jews or those who will hand over the entire past to generations to come. We will either forfeit or enrich the legacy of ages.

To Forget

The gravest sin for a Jew
is to forget what he represents.

Dawn and Dusk

We are God's stake in human history. We are the dawn and the dusk, the challenge and the test. How strange to be a Jew and to go astray on God's perilous errands. We have been offered as a pattern of worship and as a prey for scorn, but there is more still in our destiny. We carry the gold of God in our souls to forge the gate of the kingdom. The time for the kingdom may be far off, but the task is plain: to retain our share in God in spite of peril and contempt. There is a war to wage against the vulgar, against the glorification of the absurd, a war that is incessant, universal. Loyal to the presence of the ultimate in the common, we may be able to make it clear that man is more than man, that in doing the finite he may perceive the infinite.

Mission to the Jews

The mission to the Jews is a call to betray . . . the sacred history of their people. Very few Christians seem to comprehend what is morally and spiritually involved in supporting such activities. We are Jews as we are men. The alternative to our existence as Jews is spiritual suicide, extinction. It is not a change into something else. Judaism has allies but no substitutes.

The . . . marvel of Jewish existence, the survival of holiness in the history of the Jews, is a continuous verification of the marvel of the Bible. Revelation to Israel continues as a revelation through Israel.

The Protestant pastor, Christian Furchtegott Gellert, was asked by Frederick the Great, "Herr Professor, give me proof of the Bible, but briefly, for I have little time." Gellert answered, "Your Majesty, the Jews." . . .

Gustave Weigel spent the last evening of his life in my study at the Jewish Theological Seminary. We opened our hearts to one another in prayer and contrition and spoke of our own deficiencies, failures, hopes. At one moment I posed the question: Is it really the will of God that there be no more Judaism in the world? Would it really be the triumph of God if the scrolls of the Torah would no more be taken out of the Ark and the Torah no more read in the Synagogue, our ancient Hebrew prayers, in which Jesus himself worshipped, no more recited, the Passover Seder no more celebrated in our lives, the law of Moses no more observed in our homes? Would it really be *ad majorem Dei gloriam* to have a world without Jews?

Jew and Christian

The problem to be faced is: how to combine loyalty to one's own tradition with reverence for different traditions? How is mutual esteem between Christian and Jew possible?

A Christian ought to ponder seriously the tremendous implications of a process begun in early Christian history. I mean the conscious or unconscious dejudaization of Christianity, affecting the Church's way of thinking, its inner life as well as its relationship to the past and present reality of Israel— the father and mother of the very being of Christianity. The children did not arise to call the mother blessed; instead, they called the mother blind. Some theologians continue to act as if they did not know the meaning of "honor your father and mother"; others, anxious to prove the superiority of the church, speak as if they suffered from a spiritual Oedipus complex.

A Christian ought to realize that a world without Israel will be a world without the God of Israel.

THE LAND

We Are a Harp

We have arrived at a beginning; the night often looked interminable. Amalek was Führer, and Haman prevailed.

For centuries we would tear our garments whenever we came into sight of your ruins. In 1945 our souls were ruins, and our garments were tatters. There was nothing to tear. In Auschwitz and Dachau, in Bergen-Belsen and Treblinka, they prayed at the end of Atonement Day, "Next year in Jerusalem." The next day they were asphyxiated in gas chambers. Those of us who were not asphyxiated continued to cling to Thee. "Though he slay me, yet I will trust in him" (Job 13:15). We come to you, Jerusalem, to build your ruins, to mend our souls and to seek comfort for God and men.

We, a people of orphans, have entered the walls to greet the widow, Jerusalem, and the widow is a bride again.

She has taken hold of us, and we find ourselves again at the feet of the prophets.

We are the harp, and David is playing.

The State of Israel

Why was Mount Moriah chosen to be the site on which to build the Temple and the Holy of Holies rather than Mount Sinai on which the Ten Commandments were given? The answer offered is that Mount Moriah was the site where Abraham sacrificed his beloved son and the sanctity of sacrifice transcends the sanctity of the Commandments.

Infinitely greater than the sacrifice of Isaac was the martyrdom of Auschwitz, Bergen-Belsen, Dachau, Treblinka, and others. The State of Israel was built on that martyrdom; its people are, to use a phrase of the prophet Zechariah (3:2), "a brand plucked from the fire."

The Holy Land

We are tired of explusions, of pogroms; we have had enough of extermination camps. We are tired of apologizing for our existence. If I should go to Poland or Germany, every stone, every tree would remind me of contempt, hatred, murder, of children killed, of mothers burned alive, of human beings asphyxiated.

When I go to Israel every stone and every tree is a reminder of hard labor and glory, of prophets and psalmists, of loyalty and holiness. The Jews go to Israel not only for physical security for themselves and their children; they go to Israel for renewal, for the experience of resurrection.

Is the State of Israel God's humble answer to Auschwitz? A sign of God's repentance for men's crime of Auschwitz?

No act is as holy as the act of saving human life. The Holy Land, having offered a haven to more than two million Jews—

113

many of whom would not have been alive had they remained in Poland, Russia, Germany, and other countries—has attained a new sanctity.

Jerusalem

The words have gone out of here
and have entered the pages of holy books.
And yet Jerusalem has not given herself away.
There is so much more in store. . .
She is the city where waiting for God was born,
where the anticipation of everlasting peace came
    into being.
Jerusalem is waiting for new beginning.

What is the secret of Jerusalem?
Her past is a prelude.
Her power is in reviving.
Her silence is prediction,
    the walls are in suspense.
It may happen any moment:
    a shoot may come forth out of the stock of Jesse,
        a twig may grow forth out of his roots.

This is a city never indifferent to the sky.
The evenings often feel like Kol Nidre nights.
Unheard music,
    transfiguring thoughts.
Prayers are vibrant.
The Sabbath finds it hard to go away.
                    • • •

Here Isaiah (6:3) heard:
Holy, holy holy is the Lord of hosts:
the whole earth is full of his glory.
No words more magnificent have ever been uttered.
Here was the Holy of Holies.

Psalms inhabit the hills,
the air is hallelujah.
Hidden harps.
Dormant songs.

An Echo of Eternity

Jerusalem!
I always try to see the inner force
that emanates from you.
I try to use my eyes, and there is a cloud.
Is Jerusalem higher than the road I walk on?
Does she hover in the air above me?
No,
in Jerusalem past is present,
and heaven is almost here.
For an instant I am near to Hillel.
All of our history is within reach.

Jerusalem, you only see her when you hear.
She has been an ear when no one else heard,
an ear open to prophets' denunciations,
    to prophets' consolations,
        to the lamentations of ages,
to the hopes of countless sages and saints;

115

an ear to prayers flowing from distant places.
And she is more than an ear.
Jerusalem is a witness,
an echo of eternity.
Stand still and listen.

We know Isaiah's voice from hearsay,
yet these stones heard him
when he said concerning Judah and Jerusalem:

> It shall come to pass in the latter days. . . .
> For out of Zion shall go forth Torah,
>   and the word of the Lord from Jerusalem.
> He shall judge between the nations,
>   and shall decide for many peoples;
> nation shall not lift up sword against nation,
>   neither shall they learn war any more. (2:2–4)

Jerusalem was stopped in the middle of her speech.
She is a voice interrupted.
Let Jerusalem speak again to our people,
to all people.

The Wall

> The Wall.
> At first I am stunned.
> Then I see a Wall of frozen tears, a cloud of sighs.
> Palimpsests, hiding books, secret names.
> The stones are seals.
> The Wall.
> The old mother crying for all of us. Stubborn, loving,

waiting for redemption. The ground on which I stand is Amen. My words become echoes. All of our history is waiting here.

No comeliness to be acclaimed, no beauty to be relished. But a heart and an ear. Its very being is compassion. You stand still and hear: stones of sorrow, acquaintance with grief. We all hide our faces from agony, shun the afflicted. The Wall is compassion, its face is open only to those smitten with grief.

Silence. I hug the stones; I pray. O, Rock of Israel, make our faith strong and Your words luminous in our hearts and minds. No image. Pour holiness into our moments.

The Wall is silent? For an instant I am her tongue. Then I hear: I am a man of unclean lips. . . . O God, cleanse my lips, make me worthy to be her tongue. Forgive me for having tried to be her tongue for one instant. Forgive my ecstasy.

I am afraid of indifference, of disjunctions. Since Auschwitz my joys grieve, pleasures are mixed with vexations.

No security anywhere, any time. The sun can be a nightmare, humanity infinitely worse than a beast. How to be in accord with Isaiah? I ask in my prayers.

Suddenly ancient anticipations are resurrected in me. Centuries went and came. Then a moment arrived and stood still, facing me.

Once you have lived a moment at the Wall, you never go away.

Mother of Israel

Jerusalem, the mother of Israel, we enter your walls as children who have always honored you, who have never been estranged from you. Your weight has been weighed in tears shed by our people for nearly two thousand years. Laughter was suppressed when we thought of your being in ruins. You are not a shrine, a place of pilgrimage to which to come, and then depart. "Wherever I go, I go to Jerusalem," said Rabbi Nahman.

List of Sources

Earth   = *The Earth Is the Lord's*
God   = *God in Search of Man*
Insecurity   = *The Insecurity of Freedom*
Israel   = *Israel: An Echo of Eternity*
Not Alone   = *Man Is Not Alone*
Prophets   = *The Prophets*
Quest   = *Man's Quest for God*
Sabbath   = *The Sabbath*
USQR   = "No Religion Is an Island," *Union Seminary Quarterly Review* 21, no. 2, pt. 1 (1966)
Who?   = *Who Is Man?*

*From "Religion in a Free Society," which first appeared in *Religion in America: Original Essays on Religion in a Free Society*, edited by John Cogley (New York: Meridian Books, 1958), later reprinted in *The Insecurity of Freedom*.

122

ACKNOWLEDGMENTS

OF RELATED INTEREST